A very significant book, by a British economist, dealing in a highly intelligent fashion with one of the most important issues of our times – the causes of wage inflation. After surveying various "monocausal" theories, and pointing out their inadequacies, Hudson proposes his own persuasive eclectic synthesis of wage setting. This is based, on the one hand, on combining search theory and implicit contracting analysis with, on the other, a realistic theory of the wage bargaining process. This leads to the establishment of both a "fair" wage (the employer's goal) and an "aspiration" wage (the worker's goal). Possible bargaining outcomes, when these two wages conflict, are explored. The application of this analysis to the differing institutional environments of the UK and the US is an illuminating feature of the book. No explicit attention is given to the formation of prices, *per se*, but the evidence that this process if "driven" by wage and productivity behavior is overwhelming. Hudson concludes that reducing wage inflation in the UK is virtually a hopeless task; whereas in the US, because of the different institutional setting, inflation fighters have some, although remote, prospect of success. The book is closely argued but its main ideas – which are extremely provocative – can be mastered by the proverbial general reader. An extensive bibliography will aid scholars. A book not to be missed by anyone interested in one of our major macroeconomic maladies!"

Choice, 1982

*Inflation: A Theoretical Survey
and Synthesis*

Inflation: A Theoretical Survey and Synthesis

JOHN HUDSON

London
GEORGE ALLEN & UNWIN
Boston   Sydney

George Allen & Unwin (Publishers) Ltd,
40 Museum Street, London WC1A 1LU, UK

George Allen & Unwin (Publishers) Ltd,
Park Lane, Hemel Hempstead, Herts HP2 4TE, UK

Allen & Unwin Inc.,
9 Winchester Terrace, Winchester, Mass 01890, USA

George Allen & Unwin Australia Pty Ltd,
8 Napier Street, North Sydney, NSW 2060, Australia

First published in 1982
Second impression 1983

British Library Cataloguing in Publication Data

Hudson, John
    Inflation.
1. Inflation (Finance)
I. Title
332.4'1   HG229
ISBN 0-04-339025-0
    0-04-339034-X Pbk

Library of Congress Cataloging in Publication Data

Hudson, John (John R.)
    Inflation, a theoretical survey and synthesis.
Bibliography: p.
1. Inflation (Finance)   I. Title.
HG229.H883   332.4'1   81-14996
ISBN 0-04-339025-0   AACR2
    0-04-339034-X Pbk

Set in 10 on 12 point Press Roman by Alden Press Ltd,
and printed and bound by Vail-Ballou Press, Inc.,
Binghamton, N.Y.

For Annie

Contents

Preface

The 1970s has seen the development of the most serious economic crisis since the 1930s. However, as with the 1930s this has led to something of a revolution in economic theory. Faced with the collapse of previously accepted ideas, economists have sought a new paradigm that would be capable of explaining the world as they now perceive it. This has led to the development of many new areas which have enriched our understanding of many aspects of that world. Unfortunately these have not combined to give us this new paradigm, to present us with a view of the world that can be accepted by most economists as providing a realistic simplification of the way that world functions. This is the task which this book sets out to perform, with respect to that part of the world associated with the labour market and in particular the way it generates inflation.

To do this it will be necessary to build upon some of these new developments — elements from search theory, implicit contract theory, theories of expectation formation, new theories of bargaining, even the permanent income hypothesis, all these will be combined into one unified theory of inflation — and in the process some contributions will be made to all of these separate areas in their own right. For example, in search theory we shall relax the assumption of a constant search productivity regardless of the state of the labour market.

There is only one area of development of the 1970s that I shall not be making use of — that concerned with the rational expectations–labour market clearing model of the monetarists. In my view this model is based upon assumptions which are totally unrealistic and has implications which are equally so. Yet it is this model which has seen the most dynamic growth in the 1970s, and which has had the most significant impact on economic policy, particularly in the UK. It is one of the tasks of this book to show why I believe this impact has essentially been destructive.

In doing this I shall examine the course and causes of inflation in both the UK and the USA. For the latter I suggest that the inflation rate should decline naturally within the course of the next decade. I further suggest that there is little that policy makers can do to speed this process up and that they would be better employed concerning themselves with other problems. This may also be the case for the UK, but for the rather different reason that inflation is a much more deep-seated problem than in the USA, and it may be that there is no solution to it within the confines of a democratic society. However, if there is one then I believe it lies within the realm of an expanding economy enjoying high productivity growth – the arrival of the microchip may have a crucial role to play here.

It is hoped that, despite the difficult tasks the book sets itself, it will be amenable to postgraduate students and advanced undergraduate students. As far as possible I have avoided the use of complicated mathematics, without giving up too much in terms of theoretical rigour. Economics should be about ideas and these should be capable of being expressed in essentially verbal terms. It is also hoped that students of monetary economics, labour economics and macroeconomics will find useful the considerable amount of material critically reviewing the literature in this area. This takes into its compass theoretical and empirical work on expectations, search theory, implicit contract theory, rational expectations, and bargaining theories.

In writing this book, which has taken several years, I have had considerable help from many people. It is a development of my PhD thesis done at Warwick University, and partially financed by the Centre for Industrial Economic and Business Research which is based there. My first supervisor was John Williamson, followed by Ben Knight. The initial stages were completed when I was at Durham University, and it was there that the embryonic version of the search theory first saw light of day in work I was doing with Joost van Doorn. More recently I have cause to thank Nicholas Brealey and Rowena Friedman of Allen & Unwin, together with three anonymous referees, whose many excellent comments I have gratefully devoured. I would also like to thank Patrick Minford who, although a monetarist and in obvious disagreement with much of the book, none the less gave me considerable encouragement.

Finally I would like to thank my wife Annie, who has been faced with the daunting task of keeping two small children out of my way while I have been writing this book, and for her considerable help and encouragement.

JOHN HUDSON

Chapter 1
Theories of Inflation

Within economics there have grown up two main approaches to inflation. First, the mainstream view regards it as, for want of a better phrase, an excess demand phenomenon. The alternative is to see it in terms of a bargaining situation between bilateral monopolists — employers on the one side and trade unions on the other. In this case, although the forces of supply and demand may influence the outcome, they may not be the most important factors with, for example, the degree of union militancy taking a principal role. We shall begin by examining the development of the mainstream approach and then turn to bargaining theories.

Excess Demand Theories of Inflation

The possible existence of a relationship between inflation and excess demand has long been realised; for example, Joseph Lowe (1822) assigned a causal role to both supply and demand factors when discussing the inflation associated with the Napoleonic wars. In particular he listed the extra demand for men for government service as causing an increase in wages and salaries. In the twentieth century attention has focused on the specific form of this relationship which links unemployment with inflation. One of the earliest works which explicitly postulated such a relationship was Fisher's 1926 paper. Fisher took the rate of change of prices as the independent variable; in other words, the causation runs from price changes to unemployment. In his model an increase in prices preceded an increase in such contractual costs as wages, thereby stimulating employment, for a short time at least.

In more recent times interest in such a relationship stems, not from Fisher, but from Phillips's classic paper (1958), where, to quote Friedman (1975), he 'rediscovered' this relationship. This rediscovery consisted of fitting a curve through observations in the unemployment–wage inflation plane for the period 1861 to 1913; when he came to compare more recent observations with this curve he found a 'stunning correspondence'. He also found that actual observations tended to loop around this curve in, usually, an anticlockwise direction. Thus if unemployment was falling, the rate of wage inflation would be higher than that indicated by the curve and vice versa if unemployment was rising. Phillips's rationale for these loops was not made entirely clear, although Lipsey (1960) thought that he might have had some expectational mechanism in mind, whereby employers might vary the strength of their bidding not merely in response to present needs, but because of expected future needs. However, as Lipsey also noted, there are certain difficulties with this and other possible explanations, and finding a rationale for these loops became a favoured pastime for economists for several years.

Finally, Phillips postulated a restricted role for price increases, which operates with a threshold effect. It is only when the cost of living rises more rapidly than money wages that these become operative. He argued that when this was not the case, that is, when money wages are rising more rapidly than the cost of living, then employers will merely be giving under the name of cost of living adjustments part of the increases they would in any case have given as a result of their competitive bidding for labour. This hypothesis has not received much attention, nor been further developed, and Trevithick and Mulvey (1975), for example, find it 'not particularly convincing'. However, it seems to me a hypothesis worth further consideration, particularly in how it links up with more recent developments.

One important implication of Phillips's work is that it indicates the existence of a trade-off between unemployment and inflation. For example, the curve showed that at a rate of unemployment of about 2.5 per cent wages would rise at about 2 per cent p.a., which is consistent with price stability if productivity is also rising at 2 per cent. A lower level of unemployment could then only be achieved at the cost of inflation. The existence of this trade-off generated a great deal of literature, particularly on the optimal combination of unemployment and inflation.

Although it is clear that Phillips had in mind the hypothesis that wage inflation is a function of excess demand in the labour market, there was little in the way of theoretical justification for this. This had to wait until Lipsey's paper, which, basically, for the case of a single micro-labour market, postulated a wage reaction function dependent upon the ratio of excess demand for labour to total supply. He then linked the rate of unemployment with this ratio, and upon combining the two relationships obtained an additional one between wage inflation and unemployment. Lipsey's explanation of the loops was simply that in the upswing some labour markets might lag behind others, pushing the Phillips curve to the right, while in the downswing the lag disappears and hence the macro-curve coincides with the micro-curves. Ingenious as it is this explanation suffers from a number of flaws. First, relatively little in the way of justification is given for the operation of the lags in this manner. Secondly, it assumes identical micro-reaction curves, an assumption which has been called into question by Bowers *et al.* (1970) and Sargan (1971).

An alternative explanation for the loops, which can be made compatible with the rest of Lipsey's theory, was put forward by Hines (1971). He proposed that job vacancies and unemployment are not related in any simple linear way, but that when excess demand is rising vacancies will rise more rapidly than unemployment falls, and vice versa when excess demand is falling. Thus unemployment will understate the true level of excess demand when it is rising and overstate it when it is falling. Hines argued that a valid proxy for excess demand is provided by the level of unemployment together with its rate of change. This then would seem to offer an explanation for the loops which suffers from none of the drawbacks of either Phillips's or Lipsey's.

In the USA the earliest contribution to this literature came from Samuelson and Solow (1960). They found the American Phillips curve lay slightly to the right of that of the UK, with a rate of unemployment of 5 per cent stabilising the wage rate in the UK, but leading to 2.5 per cent inflation in the USA. They also drew attention to a Phillips curve with prices and not wages on the vertical axis. This was derived from the wage-defined Phillips curve, by assuming that wage increases are fully passed on and a rate of productivity growth of 2.5 per cent p.a., and as such was compatible with Phillips's original approach. It did however set something of a precedent for future work done on the US economy, where many economists have estimated directly the relationship between price inflation and unemployment, and contrasts sharply with the UK, where wages have been the subject of most attention. This has some implications for empirical work, for if it is assumed that excess demand affects prices only through wage changes, then an exact and immediate relationship between price changes and unemployment will only emerge if wage changes are immediately passed on to prices in full. If they are not, or if there is a lag between the two, perhaps varying with economic conditions, then a price-defined Phillips curve becomes more difficult to identify.

However, this is only a relatively minor point, and it is clear that the notion of a relationship between unemployment and inflation was quickly absorbed by the economics profession on both sides of the Atlantic. As an empirical concept it seemed beyond dispute. In addition, Lipsey's analysis seemed to have provided the basis for a satisfactory theoretical explanation of the relationship. Thus, by the second half of the 1960s it was probably the opinion of the majority of the profession that the only remaining questions were essentially peripheral ones, such as those surrounding the trade-off. Unfortunately this feeling of satisfaction was rudely shattered by actual events. In the UK the Phillips curve appeared to shift substantially and unpredictably to the right in 1966–7 and again in 1969–70, this latter shift being replicated in the USA as well as many other developed countries. The years 1969–70, in particular, mark a watershed in our thinking about inflation. In both countries deflationary policies were being followed in an attempt to reduce inflation. Yet, as we shall see later, they met with little success. Unemployment increased, but with relatively little effect on inflation. In the face of these failures many economists attempted to reconstruct the Phillips curve in a way which could account for these events. This reconstruction took place on two planes, the first revolved around attempts to improve upon unemployment as a measure of excess demand. The second was more fundamental and involved a reconstruction of the theoretical framework proposed by Lipsey, which has led to what has become known as the expectations augmented Phillips curve.

In the UK, those economists who argued that unemployment was a less than adequate measure of excess demand noted that there was also an apparent shift in the relationship between unemployment and vacancies (Bowers *et al.*, 1970). Possible reasons for this shift, which implied a shift between unemployment and excess demand and hence in the Phillips curve, include the introduction of earnings related benefits in October 1966, which had the effect of almost doubling unemployment benefit payable to a man who had previously been receiving average earnings, the introduction of statutory redundancy payments in December 1965 and various labour shake-out hypotheses. Because of this it has been argued that vacancies give a more accurate measure of excess demand than unemployment. Thus Trevithick and Mulvey (1975) report that the vacancy rate performs considerably more satisfactorily than the unemployment rate as an explanatory variable in the wage equation for the years 1966–9; however, in 1970–1 this too breaks down.

In a similar vein Simler and Tella (1968) use a 'labour reserves' variable for the USA, which corrected for variations in labour force participation rates. Taylor, in a series of papers (1970, 1972 and Godfrey and Taylor, 1973), has used a measure of unemployment which includes estimates of hoarded labour. The results of such exercises are somewhat contradictory. Perry (1970) and Taylor (1970) found that including such variables in the equations for the USA did not improve the results, whereas Simler and Tella found that they did. For the UK, Taylor (1972) and Godfrey and Taylor found hoarded labour to be a significant factor, though this only seems to apply to the rate of change of earnings corrected for overtime and not to the wage rate change equation.

In recent years, interest in the USA has centred on the effects of demographic and legislative factors on unemployment. Amongst the former are the growth of the youth proportion of the labour force due to the maturing of the post-Second World War baby boom, the increase in female participation rates and the growth of multi-worker families, while on the legislative side, increases in the coverage and value of unemployment insurance have, as in the UK, been the subject of considerable analysis. All these factors will be discussed in more detail when analysing the US economy. Meanwhile we may note that although these factors may well have led to some increase in unemployment, it is unlikely that they can by themselves provide an explanation for the changes in the Phillips curve, especially the sluggish response of inflation to unemployment in recent years. This is especially the case as many of the above changes occurred gradually over time, for example the growth in female participation rates, whereas the change in the Phillips curve was relatively sudden. Thus although these factors might account for a gradual shift in the Phillips curve over time, they cannot explain what actually happened. In addition there has almost certainly been some selection bias in this whole area. Economists are aware that a level of unemployment which twenty years ago would have signalled a recession can no longer be relied upon to reduce inflation. Therefore the search has been on for factors which have tended to increase the level of unemployment. There has not been the same incentive to search for other factors which might have had the reverse effect. Some of the results of this search have made valid contributions to the literature, but others have not. The case of labour hoarding seems particularly weak. This occurs when employers keep labour in excess of their immediate requirements. They do not therefore represent a source of excess supply of labour, because their services have been bid for, and in excess demand terms it matters little as to the possible motives of the bidder, although in another context it could be argued that, as these workers are not actively engaged in productive work, the employer might not be so keen to bid for more workers as he might otherwise be. However, in this case hoarded labour would be acting as a proxy for employers' keenness to bid for labour, and it does not seem valid to place it in the equation on the same grounds as registered unemployment, which is there to represent excess demand. If hoarded labour is to be entered in the equation as a proxy for employers' keenness, then it should properly be entered as affecting the speed with which the market responds to excess demand, not as a component of excess demand itself.

The Expectations Augmented Phillips Curve

The second line of approach, aimed at rehabilitating the Phillips curve, involved a much more fundamental reappraisal of the theoretical framework proposed by Lipsey. Once again within this general reappraisal there appear to have been two fairly distinct approaches, both of which had their beginnings prior to the 1970 period which saw the shift in the Phillips curve. The first was developed by Friedman (1968), and involved a more rigorous application of the commodity market approach which lies at the root of present monetarist theories of inflation. The second saw light of day in a remarkable group of essays by, among others, Phelps (1968), Mortenson (1970) and Holt (1970). These provided the major impetus to search theories which have had a significant impact on other areas of economics besides inflation. This approach is, in some respects, more revolutionary than Friedman's, as it abandons the perfectly competitive labour market assumption made by both him and Lipsey. In addition, it is, as developed by Mortenson, for example, a dynamic theory, in the sense that decision makers are not restricted to considerations of the present alone. However, a more detailed analysis of this approach will have to wait until we have examined the contributions made by Friedman and others who have been influenced by him.

Friedman argues that the relevant wage rate in Phillips's and Lipsey's theories should be the real one and not the money one. In addition, as both potential employers and employees envisage the employment contract covering a fairly long period, it will be the anticipated real wage, not the current one, which is relevant. The Phillips curve should therefore be written as

$$\dot{W}_t - \dot{P}_t^e = f(U_t) \tag{1.1}$$

or

$$\dot{W}_t = f(U_t) + \dot{P}_t^e \tag{1.2}$$

where $\dot{W}_t$ and U_t denote the rate of wage inflation and the level of unemployment in period t, respectively, and $\dot{P}_t^e$ denotes the expected rate of price inflation over some future period related to average contract duration. This equation is known as the price expectations augmented Phillips curve. Friedman also argued that for short periods price inflation expectations might lag behind actual inflation, but that, given a constant inflation rate, expectations would eventually catch up with inflation. If the assumption is then made that in the long run the rate of price inflation equals the rate of wage inflation plus a constant, k, which may be negative, and represents the rate of productivity growth plus any other long-term effects on the inflation rate, then we can rewrite (1.2) as

$$\dot{P}_t = f(U_t) + \dot{P}_t^e - k \qquad (1.3)$$

It then follows that in the long run, if the coefficient on expectations equals unity (which is implicit in the way the equations have been presented), any long-run trade-off between unemployment and inflation disappears. In this case there is only one possible sustainable level of unemployment, which is known as the 'natural rate of unemployment', and is given by the following formula:

$$U_t = f^{-1}(k) \qquad (1.4)$$

If the employment rate is below this level then it will lead to a rate of wage inflation higher than the growth in productivity and hence to price inflation, this in turn will generate price inflation expectations which will further increase the rate of wage inflation and so on. This hypothesis has come to be called the accelerationist, or natural rate hypothesis, as a policy of trying to hold unemployment below the natural rate must lead to ever accelerating inflation. Similarly a rate of unemployment above the natural rate would lead to ever accelerating deflation. The natural rate itself will be determined by two factors, the rate of productivity growth, and the nature of the functional relationship between unemployment and inflation. This, in turn, will depend upon such factors as the efficiency with which the labour market allocates workers to job vacancies, the degree of structural unemployment, etc.

Friedman's hypothesis was originally greeted with considerable scepticism, but considerable effort was directed at testing it, with particular attention to the coefficient on the expectations variable. The chief problem in all this work has been to find a suitable measure of expectations of inflation. An early attempt was made by Solow (1969); he assumed expectations to be formed by an adaptive expectations mechanism and experimented with different parameters, choosing the most satisfactory in terms of statistical significance. He estimated the coefficient on price expectations to be about 0.4, which was significantly less than 1, and therefore concluded that there was a long-run trade-off between unemployment and inflation. Other studies followed by, among others, Lucas and Rapping (1969), Saunders and Nobay (1972), Turnovsky (1972), Parkin, Sumner and Ward (1976) and McGuire (1976). The results varied, but most found expectations to be significant. Some, for example, Parkin, Sumner and Ward, found the coefficient to be insignificantly different from 1, but this was by no means a universal conclusion. However, as the decade wore on, and more data from the 1970s were used, so the coefficient on expectations typically increased in size. Perhaps, partly because of this, the concept of a natural rate of unemployment has become increasingly accepted by economists, most of whom would now reject any notion of a long run trade-off between unemployment and inflation, although, as we shall see, this has not signalled a similar acceptance of the other elements of monetarist doctrine.

These studies tackled the problem of proxying expectations in different ways. Some generated an expectations series in a similar manner to Solow, while others used an expectations series derived from sample surveys. McGuire estimated expectations by treating them as coefficients on a dummy variable in a set of equations comprised of the Phillips curve, Fisher's nominal interest rate equation, a price change equation and a price expectation formation equation. Others have used the difference between the real and money rates of interest, and still others have used Muth's (1961) rational expectations hypothesis, which we discuss in detail in the next section, as a basis to model expectations. However, it is far from clear that any of these has been wholly successful, and the problem of proxying expectations remains one of the chief stumbling blocks to empirical work in this area.

One possible reason why the coefficient on expectations might not be unity is that price inflation below a certain level may be too small to be perceived, or that though perceived is too small to make adjustments for in the labour market. This argument was made by Eckstein and Brinner (1972), on the grounds that in 'normal times', defined as any period when consumer prices have risen on average by no more than 2.5 per cent p.a. over the previous two years, workers perceive and experience relatively little wage reduction. Consequently they have little incentive, when bargaining with employers, to insist on obtaining money wage settlements proportionate to their expectations of price increase. Johnston and Timbrell (1973) have also argued for a non-linear price expectations effect, again within the context of a bargaining model. They argue that since price expectations are a crucial determinant of the size of the real claim and the vigour with which it is pursued, it is not clear that it must enter the wage equation in a simple linear fashion. In the empirical results, which are for the UK, they find some degree of support for this hypothesis.

A rather different line of development, found in both Gordon (1971) and Parkin, Sumner and Ward (1976), is to try and include not only the general price inflation expectations, which are relevant to the average worker, but also product price expectations, which are the main concern of employers. Parkin, Sumner and Ward include three measures of price inflation expectations, one set relating to consumer prices and two others with specific relevance to employers, one for domestic and a second for export prices. It is worth noting that employers' expectations seem to be the most important, in that the sum of the two expectational terms relating to them is around 0.7, and that concerning consumers is about 0.3.

Friedman's paper was slightly ambiguous in one important sense. At times it seems as though he accepts that wage inflation is a function of unemployment along the lines suggested by Lipsey and Phillips. He talks, for example, of a lower level of unemployment (than the natural rate) being an 'indication that there is excess demand for labour that will produce upward pressure on real wage rates.' However, later his discussion suggests what was to become one of the basic pillars of the 'new classical macroeconomics', namely, faith in the Walrasian auctioneer's ability to clear the labour market. Unemployment only fluctuates from the natural rate if workers incorrectly forecast the price level.

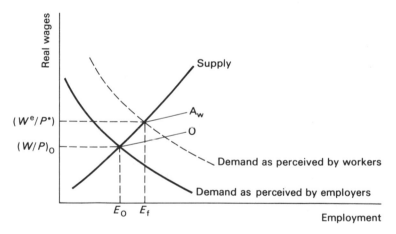

Figure 1.1   *Demand and supply in the labour market*

However, by 1977 the ambiguity had been removed, and apparently forgotten. Friedman points out that in Fisher's earlier paper the direction of causality was from inflation to unemployment. He compares this with the analyses made by Phillips and Lipsey, and concludes that the fallacy lay with them. The essence of the argument is as follows. In Figure 1.1 (W/P_0) is the equilibrium real wage, and initially he assumes a constant price level. Now let something produce a widespread increase in nominal demand, which leads employers to seek to hire more workers. As the workers have no reason to anticipate a change in the price level they will interpret the increased wage offer as an increase in real wages. They will then move along their supply curve to A_w, where (W^e/P^*) denotes the real wage as perceived by the worker, it is actually less than this, and E_f the new, increased level of employment. This situation is only temporary, as employees come to recognise that prices in general have risen, and slide back down their supply curve from A_w to 0.

Thus the causal linkage in this analysis is from something increasing demand, and thus prices, to an increase in nominal wages and employment, producing a reduction in unemployment. Hence he appears to be criticising the Phillips–Lipsey framework in as much as unemployment is not a valid proxy for excess demand in the labour market. Thus the difference between the two sides is whether excess demand affects wages or prices first. In the Keynesian model it is wages which then affect prices, while in the monetarist model it is the other way round. In this latter case the correct specification of the Phillips curve is

$$U_t = U_n + f(W_t^e - W_t^n) \qquad (1.5)$$

where W_t^e is the workers' real wage as they perceive it and W_t^n is the real wage consistent with the natural rate of unemployment. This is then made dynamic by the argument that W_t^e can only differ from W_t^n if workers' expectations about future price levels, and hence the expected rate of inflation, are wrong. If over the period for which the wage is to be effective workers underestimate the rate of inflation, they will overestimate the real wage being offered by the employer. A greater level of employment, and hence a lower level of unemployment, will then be the result. If workers' expectations are correct, however, then they will judge the value of the nominal wage offer correctly, in which case the two curves will intersect at 0. Thus equation (1.5) is more often rewritten as

$$U_t = U_n + f(\dot{P}_t - \dot{P}_t^e) \qquad (1.6)$$

The 'something' which increases nominal demand is of course an increase in the money supply. More specifically it is argued that the rate of price inflation is a lagged function of changes in the money supply, that is,

$$\dot{P}_t = g(\dot{M}_t, \dot{M}_{t-1}, \ldots) \qquad (1.7)$$

the theoretical justification for this coming from the quantity theory. The wage equation is more seldom specified, but presumably contains lagged price inflation terms. In the long run, ignoring productivity growth, the two must grow at the same rate. In the short run they may differ.

There are however difficulties with this theory. First, as we have seen, price increases should predate increases in wages. Yet the evidence seems to be that, in both the US and the UK, wages tend to lead prices. This is perhaps not too serious. The model could be reformulated in terms of employers paying higher wages in anticipation of higher selling prices. But the story is then not entirely convincing, and I feel the Phillips–Lipsey approach whereby inflation is basically a labour market phenomenon fits the facts better.

Perhaps even more serious, and this criticism applies just as well to Lipsey, the labour market clearing approach can tell us little about unemployment. The whole basis of the labour market clearing framework is that when demand equals supply there are no unsatisfied buyers or sellers and prices will therefore remain stable. Yet we know that the market never clears in this way, that there are always some unemployed workers and unfilled vacancies. Friedman argues that such unemployment will result from market imperfections, information costs relating to job vacancies and labour immobility. Yet he does not provide a theoretical framework for such a result, nor explain what further modifications to the market clearing mythology these will entail. Surely this is totally invalid. If one is going to explain unemployment by reference to search costs in the labour market, then the whole of the analysis needs to be conducted within that framework.

In addition the hypothesis that unemployment is determined by a price surprise function, as in equation (1.6), is one to which many economists, myself included, find it very difficult to give any credence at all. Solow (1980), for example, finds it 'hardly plausible', is unsure as to why it should be taken seriously and knows of no convincing evidence in its favour. The basic difference here is perhaps that Lucas, Friedman and the other monetarists believe in the efficacy of the freely competitive market. They can point to general equilibrium theories which show that, under a set of assumptions, there exists a set of prices which will clear all markets. Provided therefore that prices are flexible, including wages, there is no room for excess supply in any market, including the labour market, once it is in equilibrium. Others have less faith in the competitive market. They can point to the stickiness of certain prices, or the difference between notional and effective demands within a general equilibrium framework (Malinvaud, 1977). In addition, general equilibrium analysis is essentially static. Little mention is made as to how the economy moves from one equilibrium position to another, but it is at such times, when the economy is in disequilibrium, that variations in unemployment will occur. Moreover such conditions are probably the rule rather than the exception. In conclusion, my gravest doubts at this point are not so much with the monetarist's theoretical analysis, but whether the world in which it is placed corresponds, even vaguely, to the one we live in.

Rational Expectations

The concept of rational expectations was first put forward by Muth (1961), who was in turn building upon ideas originally put forward by Modigliani and Grunberg (1954). Muth proposed that certain expectations were rational, in the sense that they were essentially the same as the predictions of the relevant, and correct, economic theory; thus implying that expectations and the event differ only by a random forecast error. This was originally proposed within the context of the decision making process of the firm, where it remained relatively unnoticed until picked up by Lucas (1972a, b) and Sargent (1973), who translated it into the field of macroeconomics in general, and inflation in particular. In this case, as expected inflation can differ from actual inflation only by a random forecast error, we can easily see, from equation (1.6), that the actual rate of unemployment also can only differ from the natural rate by a random forecast error. Moreover the government is powerless to systematically influence the level of unemployment, as any policy initiatives it takes can be correctly forecast and allowed for. The government can only affect the rate of unemployment if it acts unpredictably. This result is at the core of modern monetarist thinking, and justifies the much publicised conclusion that government policy is essentially impotent.

Not surprisingly this whole concept has been the subject of much discussion, with a great volume of literature growing up in a remarkably short space of time. Indeed it is no exaggeration to say that this probably represents the most important theoretical innovation in macroeconomics in the last decade. Besides the original contributions by Lucas and Sargent, important contributions have also been made, for example, by Sargent and Wallace (1973, 1975, 1976), Barro (1976, 1977) and McCallum (1976). Much of this literature has been concerned with testing equation (1.6) or its output equivalent. The most obvious way to do this is to test whether unemployment is related to its own past values. If it is then either the error term is unlikely to be random, or alternatively, the equation has been mispecified. Hall (1975) has done this for the USA for the period 1954–74, regressing unemployment on its own lagged values for two quarters. He found that only 1.7 per cent of the variation remained un-explained. Hall then came to the rather surprising conclusion that 98.3 per cent of the variance must have been due to shifts in the natural rate of unemployment, a conclusion both Gordon (1977b) and Shiller (1978) find difficult to accept.

Partly in response to the presence of autocorrelation in unemployment Lucas (1975) and Sargent (1976a) have argued that equation (1.6) should be modified to include lagged unemployment. This preserves government impotency, but their results imply a somewhat lengthy time lag of between three and seven years. The theoretical justification for such lags put forward by Lucas rested on information lags and serially correlated movements in capital stock. The information lags arise when an initial shock to the system causes economic agents to underestimate the true stock of money, which in turn causes them to underestimate the price level. Agents catch on to the true stock of money at an exponential rate through time, but during this catch-up period both sets of expectations lag behind. Then through a somewhat complex chain of events, the rate of interest, the demand for money and the price level itself are all affected. The net effect is that the price level will be below its equilibrium level, and government spending, which in money terms equals the increase in the money supply, will be above its equilibrium real level, thus causing an increase in output and a reduction in unemployment away from their equilibrium levels.

This reformulation of the rational expectations–natural rate hypothesis has been tested by Sargent by regressing unemployment on its own lagged values in addition to current and lagged values of another variable publicly known at time t. In this form the test is equivalent to the causality test proposed by Granger (1969). If the coefficients of the additional variable are significant then we could reject the Lucas–Sargent reformulation. Sargent uses quarterly postwar US data with real government surplus, real or money government expenditure and the price level as the extra explanatory variables, all of which are insignificant at the 5 per cent level. But when the money supply or the wage index is used, the coefficients are significant at this level. However, when he uses a similar procedure – the Sims causality test – none of these variables are significant, thus overall the results are somewhat inconclusive. In any case, in a later paper (Sargent, 1976b) he recanted upon this earlier work, claiming that due to potential correlation between the lagged independent variables and a serially correlated error term, a spurious significance might be attributed to the independent variables, thus invalidating the causality test.

An alternative approach, pursued separately by Fischer (1977), Phelps and Taylor (1977) and Taylor (1979), attributes the autocorrelation to sticky prices. According to Fischer, non-indexed labour contracts set wages in relation to expected future prices over the duration of the contract. If prices turn out to be lower than expected, real wages rise and employers may lay off workers and reduce output. More recently still we have the contribution by Brunner, Cukierman and Meltzer (1980), who argue that changes in the economic environment can be divided into permanent and transitory components, which cannot be known in advance, and are not revealed for some time after they occur. Individuals' decisions depend upon beliefs about the permanent values; for example, in the labour supply function, workers compare the currently prevailing wage, W_t, to the wage they currently perceive as permanent, W_t^p. *Ceteris paribus*, a decrease in W_t or an increase in W_t^p will reduce the current supply of labour. They then define unemployment as the difference between labour supply when W_t equals W_t^p and labour supply when the two wage rates differ. Now suppose there is a permanent fall in productivity; they argue that this will not immediately be perceived as permanent, and the unemployed will seek work at a real wage W_t^p that is not fully adjusted to the new conditions. They will therefore reject offers of employment at the current wage. These misconceptions will continue for some time, as in their model perceptions of permanent variables are based on lagged values of that variable in an adaptive manner. Thus, as with Lucas, they have a model which, although based on rational expectations, produces output and employment fluctuations, through perceptions formed in an adaptive manner lagging behind reality.

A rather different approach has been adopted by Mullineaux (1980a), who explores a suggestion by Friedman (1977) that increased variability of inflation, or anticipated inflation, may raise the natural rate of unemployment by reducing the efficiency of the price system and the market economy. Mullineaux therefore adds to equation (1.6) a measure of present and lagged uncertainty concerning expectations, one such measure being the standard deviations from the cross-section of inflation forecasts in the Livingstone surveys of expected price inflation in America. These are bi-annual surveys carried out amongst American business and academic economists concerning, amongst other things, expected price levels in the future. He also used the Livingstone data on expectations to calculate the forecasting error, which was then entered directly into the equation as an explanatory variable. His results do lend some support to Friedman's original suggestion, although in evaluating this evidence it should be borne in mind that the validity of the Livingstone data is open to question, as we shall see later. It is also worth noting that he effectively proxies the natural rate of unemployment as a lagged function of unemployment, on the grounds that this casts the test within the Granger-causality framework.

In a similar manner Barro (1977) tested a model in which forecasting errors in the money supply, rather than prices, determine unemployment. He regressed the money supply on lagged data and used the residuals as independent variables in annual regressions explaining $\log(U_t/1 - U_t)$ and output. For the sample period 1946–73 he showed that current and lagged forecast errors, together with a variable to allow for the effects of the draft, could explain 81 per cent of the variance in the unemployment term, with the coefficients on all four error terms having the correct sign. He then re-worked the regressions with the current and lagged changes in the money supply as additional explanatory variables. According to the neutrality hypothesis, the only effects of these variables should be through their unanticipated components, which are already included in the regression as forecast errors. The insignificance of the monetary variables in Barro's equation therefore supports this hypothesis.

How then are we to evaluate the contribution of the rational expectations literature to economic theory? The first point that should be made is that it has gained a lot of adherents among macro-economists, not all of whom are monetarists, within a relatively short space of time. Thus, we find in Buiter (1980), who would not lay claim to the title monetarist, a defence of rational expectations, on the grounds that any alternative expectations scheme will yield systematic errors, and that sensible economic agents will eventually abandon such a scheme. However, the claim in McCallum (1979) that some kind of consensus is emerging, which accepts the validity of rational expectations, is surely an exaggerated one. We have, for example, Laidler (1981), who does lay claim to being a monetarist and who finds rational expectations untenable, preferring to call those who do subscribe to its validity neo-Austrians rather than monetarists. My own position is close to Laidler's on this issue, and will be expanded upon in Chapter 3. I do not believe that job searchers, factory workers or even the average businessman form their expectations in this manner. I do not believe that they know the structural equations, the parameter values and the values of the variables necessary to do the calculations. It is even more difficult to believe that these all-wise factory workers from Pittsburgh or Sheffield were using a monetarist model to predict inflation in the 1950s long before economists had stumbled upon it. Of course these arguments are not new They have been, for example, hinted at by both McCallum and Buiter, yet neither seems to regard them as important. Thus, to McCallum the relevant question was not whether expectations are actually formed rationally, but whether it would be fruitful to conduct stabilisation analysis under any other assumption. This is surely wrong — expectations either are or are not formed according to the rational expectations mechanism. If they are not, then they must be formed in some other manner, and it is the job of economists to try and identify it.

Of course unrealistic assumptions can be justified on the grounds that they simplify the problem and yield insights into economic behaviour which are valuable. This does not seem to be the case for the rational expectations hypothesis. It was originally introduced in connection with the natural rate hypothesis, and yielded the result that governments were impotent to affect the level of unemployment, even in the short term. Theories are seldom arrived at in isolation from real world events, and the difficulties governments experienced in the early 1970s in reducing inflation, and later, in some cases, in restimulating the economy, were probably instrumental in the development of a theory that had at its core the implication of government policy impotency. That it developed at Chicago reflects the attraction of such a theory for the orthodox conservative tradition which had become established there. Unfortunately the theory carried with it the additional implication, which was totally at variance with our knowledge of the real world, that unemployment could only deviate from its natural rate by a stochastic error term. Monetarists were then faced with three choices: they could attempt to explain variations in unemployment as reflecting variations in the natural rate, as Hall did, or they could attempt to amend it so as to yield results compatible with real world evidence, but without changing it in any fundamental manner, or they could abandon it, as Laidler has done. The majority of monetarists took the second route, the results of which we have been examining.

In evaluating these results we must ask whether a bad theory can give birth to a good one? It is not enough to claim that the theories are valid because they produce realistic assumptions — they were designed to do so. One is reminded here of the reaction of medieval astronomers who believed that the earth was at the centre of the universe, around which all other heavenly bodies revolved. When observations revealed that these bodies followed a path inconsistent with this belief, astronomers instead of abandoning it in search of some other theory argued that these bodies followed a looping orbit around the earth. As further evidence became available, so the loops became more intricate; the theory was always consistent with reality. But how much simpler and more believable was the Copernican alternative, that the sun was at the centre of the solar system. This analogy should tell us that it will probably be difficult to decide on the validity of this theory on empirical evidence alone. As new evidence appears so the theory can be modified to be consistent with that evidence. In addition conflicting results often arise from apparently similar tests applied to the same data. Much more work needs to be done before any kind of general pattern can be seen to have emerged. Not that the evidence to date has been particularly convincing. Too often it is based on suspect data, as with Mullineaux, or uses suspect methodology, as with Sargent. For the moment then there is no choice but to use one's judgement. We must look at the two basic tenets of the rational expectations–Walrasian market clearing paradigm. We must examine the conclusion, common to all these theories, that governments cannot affect unemployment, and we must decide whether these correspond to the world as we know it.

It is clear that these theories have had an enormous influence, not just on the way economists think, but also on government policy, particularly in the UK. Indeed so great has been their influence that in some respects they represent the most important work since Keynes. Their appeal lies partly in the eloquence, the fervour and the ability of those who have been propounding them, partly in the backlash by economists and politicians, disillusioned at the failures of governments in the 1970s, and partly in their appeal to rationality and a natural order. But I believe that this approach has been counter-constructive. It has led economists out of the real world, back into the ivory towers they inhabited before Keynes.

The Keynesian Position

One further reason for the rapid growth of monetarist doctrines may be that the Keynesians, who might be seen as the natural opponents to the monetarists, have been in a state of some confusion in the 1970s. The central element to their theories on inflation has consistently been that it is essentially a labour market phenomenon. Wage inflation is determined by excess demand in the labour market together with expectations of inflation, as in equation (1.2). This then determines the rate of price inflation via a fairly constant mark-up mechanism. Faced with the changing relationship between unemployment and inflation in the 1970s, their position has become steadily less credible. Some, mainly based in the UK, have responded by moving towards wage bargaining models, viewing the breakdown of the Phillips curve as reflecting increased social divisions and union worker militancy. Others, mainly in America, have attempted to rescue their position by arguing that there is still a relationship between unemployment and inflation, but the lags are longer than had hitherto been thought, thus making it more difficult to identify. Let us take the

American position first, beginning with Gordon. In 1970 he set out a standard Phillips curve model which underpredicted the rate of inflation in the last two quarters of that year by an average of 1.1 percentage points at an annual rate. In 1971 he admitted this was a mistake and attempted to salvage the model by introducing three new measures of unemployment, disguised unemployment, unemployment of hours and unemployment dispersion, where unemployment of hours measured deviations of actual hours worked per week from an estimate of hours that would be worked at full employment. It is difficult to think of a rationale for either of these improving unemployment as a measure of excess demand. Disguised unemployment relates to marginal workers and it is hard to accept that they should be given equal weight as the officially unemployed in a proxy for excess demand, the latter presumably having a much greater commitment to the workforce. There seems even less justification for the unemployment of hours variable, unless as a proxy for employer keenness when bidding in the labour market. The labour market dispersion variable has more validity, being there due to the convex nature of the Phillips curve. Price expectations are also included in the regression, proxied by a distributed lag on past price changes. An additional price variable is the rate of change of product prices. Further, short-term factors include increases in personal and social security taxes, which shift the labour supply curve upwards, thereby increasing the equilibrium wage rate.

Gordon concluded that the fundamental problem in 1968–9 was excess demand, but temporary effects were also caused by the social security tax increase of 1966 and the personal tax surcharge of 1968–9. In addition, easier labour market conditions in 1970 did not moderate the rate of inflation because of long lags in the wage–price process, by which he apparently meant consumer price inflation expectations. Six years later Gordon (1977a) stood by these earlier results, which he felt had fully explained the course of inflation in the USA in the intervening years. On examination, however, the results appear somewhat different. Consumer price inflation expectations are no longer significant, neither are tax rates or unemployment dispersion. Furthermore, a dummy variable, included to reflect the effects of price and wage controls, is significant and considerably improves the accuracy of the regression in this period. However, as it is positive, Gordon concludes that the effect of controls on wages must have been to increase them above what they would otherwise have been. An alternative possibility is that as his equations generally underpredict the rate of wage inflation throughout the period 1970–3, the dummy variable may merely have been picking up some of this effect.

Perry (1978) also argues that wages respond to the tightness of labour markets, but not by enough to avoid fluctuations in employment brought about by corresponding fluctuations in demand — hence the Phillips curve relationship. In the empirical work he reaffirms the importance of unemployment, corrected for demographic changes, in the wage equation, and finds a significant role for lagged inflation, which has been increasing over time. He argues that this is more consistent with a backward looking effect of inflation on wages, rather than a forward looking one as with expectational models. This then introduces considerable inertia in the reaction of inflation to unemployment. However, in this paper he neither provides a satisfactory theoretical explanation for these effects, nor for their increased importance. Furthermore, as Bailey noted when discussing Perry's paper, the wage equation underpredicts the rate of inflation in every year from 1971 to 1977, and gives a cumulative underprediction of over 16 per cent. Finally the 1970 wage explosion is explained by catch-up factors which do not fit in well with the rest of the theory.

In a later paper Perry (1980) develops the inertia theme, in arguing for a normal rate of wage increase, which he derives from the implicit contract literature we shall be examining later. This 'norm' describes the trend of wage behaviour independent of real demand effects, and is the wage increase that is expected to maintain the employer's position vis-à-vis other employers. The norm is not insulated from demand conditions but responds very slowly and is also related in an adaptive manner to previous rates of increase. It may also be affected by other factors, such as oil price increases. It is the existence of this norm which explains the sluggishness of inflation in responding to demand conditions. It operates in addition to a cyclical component of wage inflation which does respond quickly to demand conditions. He further argues that the norm increased in the 1970s, thus explaining the increase in inflation which occurred during that decade. However, there are difficulties with the model. The jump in the norm is not satisfactorily explained, whereas in the empirical work it is proxied by the use of dummy variables, one each for the 1950s and 1970s. Thus the norm was supposedly constant in each decade.

A third paper by Mitchell (1978) examines wage inflation using union contract data for the period 1954–76, tending towards a wage bargaining explanation. He concludes that both union and non-union sectors exhibit some, but not much, sensitivity to unemployment. He throws no real light on why the Phillips curve relationship has changed, but points to the fact that longer contract durations are likely to reduce the sensitivity of inflation to unemployment. Yet this, by itself, is unlikely to provide a full explanation of the change in the Phillips curve.

These three papers all relate to the USA. They are not necessarily classic or definitive papers, but they do illustrate the difficulty Keynesians (broadly defined) have had in maintaining a credible position. Perhaps the real test of a theory is how well it can predict the future, and on this count theirs undoubtedly fail. The failure of unemployment to reduce inflation in 1970–1 took them by surprise, and they have struggled to come to terms with it ever since.

The position taken by British Keynesians, or perhaps more exactly the new Cambridge school, is at the same time both more and less credible than their American counterparts. It is more credible because it is at least consistent with events in the UK since 1970. It is less credible because it cannot explain inflation prior to that; neither can it explain the American experience. Finally it has relatively little grounding in economic theory. It can best be explained by describing the views of the Cambridge economic policy group (CEPG). Cripps and Godley (1976) in setting out the views of this group argue that money wage determination can be represented as the outcome of periodic negotiated wage settlements composed in part of compensation for past price and tax changes and in part of ex ante changes in the disposable real wage. In particular they conceive wage bargaining as establishing an ex ante disposable real wage on the basis of taxes and prices that prevail at the time of the settlement. Important in this view is the concept of a target real wage which determines the union's ex ante disposable real wage claim. The factors which determine this target real wage are left somewhat vague, indeed they argue that they cannot be formulated with any real precision. One point on which they are certain is that unemployment does not perceptibly influence it nor the actual wage negotiated.

The concept of a target real wage also plays an important role in the explanation advocated by Henry, Sawyer and Smith (1976), which has recently been incorporated by that bastion of British Keynesianism, the National Institute of Economic and Social Research, in their macro-economic model of the UK economy. In many respects the approach by Henry, Sawyer and Smith and the CEPG appear identical, although the former pay more attention to the determination of the target real wage. They find their inspiration in an hypothesis originally developed by Sargan (1964) that trade unions bargain for real wages, but that the means to achieve a real wage claim is to strive for a particular money wage increase in the light of expected price developments. This target wage may in theory be affected by the prevailing level of unemployment reflecting the effects of excess demand or the bargaining strength of unions. As with the CEPG they use real wages or earnings net of taxes. In the empirical work they further postulate that the desired real wage grows at a constant rate, which they find to lie between 2 per cent and 2.5 per cent per annum, and tending to be higher when more recent periods are used.

They then test this model and find that it outperforms several alternatives. They conclude that the expectations augmented Phillips curve does not provide an adequate explanation of money wage changes in the UK, nor do they find any evidence of a negative relationship between unemployment and wage inflation, or support for Hines' union pushfulness which we shall be examining later. They do find 'impressive' support for their version of Sargan's model and believe that their results lend support to a trade union bargaining approach to wage inflation.

Because the real wage plays a key role in this approach it has also become known as the real wage hypothesis. It is related to recent work done in the wage bargaining area, and hints of it can also be found in work done by American economists, for example, Perry (1978) who, as we saw earlier, argued for the importance of a catch-up variable in explaining the slow response of inflation to the recession in 1970. However, there is a limit to the extent to which the theory can be used to explain inflation in the USA, since it has at its base a strong trade union movement pushing for an ever increasing standard of living. In the USA neither is the trade union movement strong enough to fit the theory, nor have real living standards been on a continual upward trend, as they have in the UK. Therefore as an explanation of inflation it is limited to the UK alone, and this must limit both its credibility and appeal.

There are other criticisms which can be made of the theory. It has rejected the existence of a UK Phillips curve not just for the 1970s, but prior to that as well. Yet if the evidence against the existence of a Phillips curve in the 1970s is fairly decisive, then the evidence in support of one prior to that is equally strong, not the least of this evidence being its almost universal acceptance by the economists of the time. What British Keynesians have provided us with therefore is a theory specific both in place and time to the UK in the 1970s. It cannot explain what caused inflation prior to that, nor can it explain why the Phillips curve broke down when it did.

Finally the theory is deficient in as much as it gives little information about the formation of the target real wage which is at the heart of the theory. The CEPG make little attempt to do so, whereas Henry, Sawyer and Smith take it to be growing at a constant rate which is not really constant, as empirical estimates tend to make it higher when more recent time periods are used. Yet what determines this rate? Has there always been such a target wage increase? If not, when and why did it come into existence? These are all points upon which the theory is silent, but they are also points which must be answered if the theory is to have any credibility.

Search Theories of Inflation and Unemployment

We noted earlier that one justification for unemployment within a market clearing framework lay in the existence of search unemployment, and it is to the literature on this that we shall now turn. Interest in search theories began with a study by Stigler (1962), which emphasised the fact that labour markets were not characterised by perfect information, and that individuals, in order to gain information about the market, needed to undertake search activities. Using this as a base Phelps (1968), Mortenson (1970), Holt (1970) and others produced a remarkable group of essays, which gave birth to what has become known as the 'new micro-economic approach to macro-economics'. Much of this work is aimed at providing a theory consistent with the simultaneous occurrence of unemployed workers and unfilled vacancies, as well as a negative relationship between wage changes and unemployment.

The gist of Phelps' theory is that, given a constant differential between a firm's wage rate and wages paid by other firms, a fall in the unemployment rate will tend to increase quits. At a sufficiently high quit rate the firm will want to increase the differential between the wage it pays and the average wage paid elsewhere. Thus, one role of unemployment in this theory stems from its effects on quit rates, rather than any supposed underbidding for jobs by unemployed workers, as often seems implicit in some market clearing analyses. The number of vacancies will also be relevant, as the more vacancies the firm has the more anxious it will be to fill them; in addition vacancies may affect quits. Hence the desired differential will be a function of the level of unemployment and the number of vacancies. The actual rate of wage change is then a constant proportion of the average desired differential. If we also take into account that wage contracts may last for some time into the future, then in setting this differential the employer will take into account expected future labour market conditions as well as present ones. Therefore, as with Friedman's model, expectations play a major role. However, the relevant expectations are not about prices, as in Friedman's model, for Phelps believes that inflationary price expectations affect money wages only through their effect on expected vacancy and unemployment rates. Given these, a rise in the expected rate of inflation will have little or no effect upon the wage increases that a firm grants, provided that it expects other firms to hold the line over the money wages they pay. In Phelps' world it is, therefore, expectations of wage inflation, with a unit coefficient, which enter the wage equation, in order to maintain the desired differential over the wages others are expected to pay, the other variables in this equation being unemployment and vacancies.

Holt is also concerned with providing a theoretical basis for the Phillips curve. In doing this he pays slightly more attention to the specific problems of search than Phelps. Important in this context is the concept of an aspiration, or acceptance, wage which declines with the length of search. If the wage at which a job is offered to a specific worker is above his acceptance wage, then he will accept the job, if not, he will refuse it. Holt assumes that the wage from his last job is the initial reference for setting the acceptance wage, but that this is adjusted to take account of the worker's initial perception of his job opportunities. For example, when the labour market is tight, workers may reasonably raise their initial aspirations, information on the job market being conveyed by such factors as the number of vacancies, the duration of unemployment that other workers have experienced, and the wages that are being offered. Thus for an individual worker, the longer he is unemployed, the lower his acceptance wage will be. Holt then assumes that the wage the worker is hired at will vary directly with his acceptance wage, and hence inversely with the time he has been unemployed.

It follows from this that, upon aggregation, the average rate of change of wages between jobs, for all workers passing through the market, varies inversely with the average duration of unemployment. To obtain a Phillips curve relation from this, Holt links the average duration of unemployment to the number of unemployed workers, proposing that the two vary directly. Hence, we get a relationship between the average rate of change of wages between jobs and the level of unemployment. To obtain the average rate of change for all workers, he also examines those workers who search and obtain jobs while still employed, and those who obtain wage changes while remaining in the same job, because of a potential quit threat. Both of these problems are handled in a similar vein to that of unemployed job searchers, and a Phillips curve emerges at the end of the analysis. It is perhaps worth noting that neither expectations of wage nor price inflation enter Holt's analysis, although they could easily be incorporated. If they were, my initial impression is that wage inflation expectations would fit most readily into the tale he told.

Like Phelps and Holt, Mortenson was concerned with providing a search theoretic rationale for the Phillips curve. Although, compared with these, he prefers to emphasise the optimisation problem facing the firm. In doing this, he makes the assumption that the job searcher acts as if he knows with certainty what his next offer will be. His optimisation problem then consists of comparing this with his current wage offer. Using this theory he then analyses the various flows in the labour market, and concludes that the rate of change in a firm's labour force depends upon the firm's own relative wage and upon the unemployment rate in the market.

Mortenson then states the ith firm's problem as one of maximising net present worth

$$V = \int_0^\infty R_i(t)e^{-rt}dt \tag{1.8}$$

where

$$R_i(t) = P_i(t)F_i(N_i(t)) - W_i(t)N_i(t) \tag{1.9}$$

and $F_i(N_i)$ is the rate of production, P_i the price, W_i the wage rate and N_i the labour force. The firm's optimal wage–employment policy is one for which the time path of W_i and N_i maximise V, subject to the rate of change of the labour force equation and the initial employment level. As a result of the problem's solution by the various firms in the market, the rate of wage inflation is found to be related to the unemployment rate, the ratio of the average product price to the average market wage, the rate of product price inflation expected by the firms in the market, the expected unemployment rate and the real interest rate.

There are several points to note here. First, the ratio of the average product price to the average market wage is relevant as it represents an improvement in the value of labour productivity relative to cost, and therefore increases the target level of employment. The real interest rate enters because there are implicit costs in adjusting the level of employment. An increase in the real interest rate reduces the incentive to incur such costs as it reduces the present value of the benefits which lie in the future. Thus, both the target level of employment and the speed of adjustment to that level are reduced. It should be noted that there are two concepts here, the target level of employment and the desired speed of adjustment. Given a constant adjustment rate, an increase in the target level of employment increases the desired rate of change of the labour force and hence the rate of inflation. Similar comments apply to an increase in the desired rate of adjustment, given a constant target employment level.

Secondly, it is the expected rate of product price inflation that Mortenson thinks is relevant. However, he makes the assumption that firms expect their own product price and the average market wage rate to inflate at the same rate; hence one could reinterpret this conclusion as implying that both sets of expectations are in fact relevant. As to the direction of causality in Mortenson's paper, both unemployment and wage inflation are endogenous variables within a simultaneous system. Thus, while the unemployment rate partially determines the desired differential of each firm, and hence the rate of inflation, changes in the unemployment rate in turn are partially determined by the difference between the actual rate of inflation and that expected by job searchers. While in Phelps and Holt the direction of causality is from the levels of unemployment and vacancies, to the desired differential and the rate of inflation (although there are hints of simultaneity here too, but these are not really emphasised). Thus it is not true, or at least not entirely true, to say, as Gordon (1977b) has, that in the Holt, Phelps and Mortenson papers the explicit line of causality is from prior wage changes to subsequent quit decision and resulting increase in unemployment.

Although a decade has passed since the appearance of these papers, there have been few significant advances in search theory since then, and it remains the case that these papers contain nearly all the relevant insights into inflation which search theories have so far provided. This may in part account for the limited impact such theories have had, for although many economists mention the importance of search in explaining unemployment, few go on to develop the argument in any detail. Much of the work that has been done concentrates on the job searcher's acceptance curve and possible reasons for its decline over time. Important here is the view developed by Telser (1973) that if the individual does not know the true distribution of wage offers, then job search provides additional information which can be used to update perceptions of that distribution in a Bayesian type adjustment process. If the individual rejects a wage offer, then it must have been below the acceptance wage when, if prior perceptions about wage offers had been correct, there would have existed the possibility that it might have exceeded it. This will lead to an adjustment of those perceptions, with a probable reduction in the acceptance wage after each period of unsuccessful search. There are two possibilities which have been developed within the literature, whereby this adjustment process can take place either before or after the offer has been considered. In the latter case Rothschild (1974) has shown, in a somewhat unlikely example, that it is conceivable that a job searcher may, somewhat paradoxically, accept a wage offer of $1, but reject one of $2.

A rather different reason for a declining acceptance wage is connected with finite time horizon models. In this case, as the search proceeds, so the benefits from further search decline, due to their being discounted over a shorter time horizon. This will then cause a reduction in the acceptance wage. However, it is doubtful as to how important this effect will actually be. First, it depends upon the assumption that workers expect to hold their next job until they retire. Secondly, for a worker with, for example, twenty years to go before retirement, earnings at retirement will be heavily discounted. An extra month's search now will therefore reduce expected discounted lifetime earnings by very little. These doubts seem to be supported by a recent cross-section study on acceptance wages by Kiefer and Neumann (1979) who found that, in general, the acceptance wage tended to rise with age, this being the opposite of what we would expect on the basis of the above arguments. Yet another reason for a declining acceptance wage has been proposed by Salop (1973), who began by modifying the original assumptions. Until now it has been assumed that individuals sample randomly from the distribution of wage offers. Salop argued that in fact job searchers usually have some information about job opportunities in different firms and that they use this to rank them. They then search systematically, starting with those firms with the best opportunities but, as the unsuccessful searcher proceeds down the list to the less likely firms, so the expected benefits of search fall, and thus his acceptance wage also falls.

A frequent criticism of search models is that they limit search to the unemployed, thus ignoring the fact that a considerable number of people change jobs without ever being unemployed. Although most search models do make this assumption, the choice between on the job and full-time search has, as we have seen, been analysed by Holt. More recently Lippman and McCall (1976), in an excellent review article, have analysed the problem. In general, it can be concluded that workers may quit because full-time search can be undertaken more intensively than on the job search, but that the costs of full-time search, including forgone income, are greater per period than on the job search. The individual will quit his job and undertake full-time search if the benefits outweigh the costs.

Another important recent development concerns what has become known as 'mismatches', and can be found in Mortenson (1977) and Wilde (1979), for example. These occur because neither employer nor employee has complete information concerning the other's characteristics at the hiring stage. The employee knows the wage rate prior to accepting a job, but is unaware of certain other nonpecuniary aspects of the job, for example, the friendliness of the workforce. Similarly, the employer has incomplete information about the worker's productivity. Mismatches occur when one of these two parties is disappointed on gaining fuller information. The resulting quits and firings are then known as 'mismatch unemployment', and form a particularly important component of youth unemployment. The young will not only be searching for information relating to conditions in a specific firm for a specific job; they will also want information concerning that job. The frequent job changes which characterise this age group can therefore be regarded as a learning mechanism by which they gain information about the type of work for which they are best suited. This is not in itself undesirable or wasteful, although a reduction in the learning period, by, for example, providing more detailed information about occupational characteristics prior to entering the labour force, would be desirable.

Wilde analyses the mismatch process by assuming that jobs are characterised by two attributes, a wage that is observed before the job is accepted, and a specific attribute that is revealed only after the job is accepted. The searcher's acceptance of a job is then conditional on the specific characteristic being above some critical value. Using this model, he analyses the effects of an increase in the time it takes to learn the value of the specific characteristic, and several conclusions emerge. First, the searcher is worse off the greater the learning time. Secondly, as the learning time increases there is a concomitant increase in the acceptance wage; in other words, when evaluation of the specific characteristic becomes more costly, it behoves the worker to spend more time acquiring a higher wage offer. Furthermore, the critical value of the specific job characteristic declines as the learning time increases, that is, once a job is provisionally accepted the probability of quitting declines with learning time.

In most search models it is assumed that workers attempt to maximise expected income. However, two recent papers by Danforth (1979) and Hall, Lippman and McCall (1979) analyse the case where job searchers maximise expected utility. Danforth reformulates the job search model to include optimal consumption behaviour, with risk averse job searchers maximising the expected utility of lifetime consumption. In a finite time horizon model his principal conclusion is that an increase in initial wealth endowments will increase the acceptance wage and hence lead to a longer expected search duration. Following on from this he shows that, within an infinite time horizon model, it may be optimal for the individual to draw down his asset holdings and hence reduce his acceptance wage over time. Thus we have yet a further reason for declining acceptance wages.

Hall, Lippman and McCall begin by considering the case where search is conducted with recall, that is, the searcher may go back and accept any previously received offer. They show that if one searcher is more risk averse than another, then his acceptance wage will be smaller. Somewhat more surprisingly they also show that for the individual the acceptance wage need not decrease as the offer distribution becomes more risky. Indeed in some cases the acceptance wage may not even exist. The explanation for this lies in the fact that in search with recall, the best offer to date acts as a kind of insurance against unsuccessful search in the future. Thus the individual may receive a high wage offer and still carry on searching. This result is, of course, reversed when search is performed without recall.

We have thus concentrated upon the employee's job search problem, and in part this reflects the emphasis in the literature. However, some theorists have followed Phelps and Mortenson in examining the employer's side of the problem. In particular, attention has been focused on how the employer estimates the potential worth of an employee. The simplest assumption is, of course, that the employer has no knowledge of this prior to hiring the worker or, alternatively, that the labour force is homogeneous. Others have argued that employers can gain information on an individual's productivity by looking for characteristics which are positively correlated with job productivity, such as education, training, dress, etc. This then gave rise to a whole volume of literature on signalling. For example, Spence (1973) has observed that this introduces incentives for individuals to devote resources to improve these characteristics, even though job productivity may not be enhanced. Lippman and McCall (1976) have argued that this will give rise to a reservation productivity; if the job searcher's signalled productivity is above this, the employer will hire him. However, this seems to ignore the possibility that the employer may be able to vary his wage offer in line with the signalled productivity of the worker. Thus a worker with a lower productivity than average may be hired at a lower wage rate. A similar argument can be made against those who argue that employers will limit their search to those sections of the population who have a general reputation for the productivity levels they are seeking.

Much of the empirical work aimed at testing job search theories has been concerned with the implications of the theory. In particular a lot of work has been done on the effects of unemployment insurance or benefits on the duration of search. As this reduces the cost of search, in terms of income forgone, it should lead to an increase in the average time spent searching and also to the wage offer eventually being accepted. Most of the empirical work supports these conclusions. In the USA Ehrenberg and Oaxaca (1976), Classen (1977) and Holen (1977) all find a small, but positive, effect of the size of weekly benefit on unemployment duration. While for the UK Cubbin and Foley (1977) and Nickell (1979) both find similar effects.

A more direct, but more difficult, approach is to attempt to quantify the effect on the acceptance wage of continuing unemployment. Both

Kasper (1967) and Stephenson (1976) find only a small effect on acceptance wages, which decline at the rate of between 0.06 and 0.4 percentage points per month. However, both of these studies, which were for the USA, are subject to selection bias, as they are based upon samples of unemployed workers. Those individuals whose acceptance wages decline slowly will, other things being equal, be less successful in search and be over-represented in the sample. Kiefer and Neumann (1979) have avoided this source of bias, although others remain in the opposite direction, and found acceptance wages to decline at the rate of 2.5 percentage points per month.

Finally Parsons (1973) applies search theory to the analysis of quit rates. He tests a variant of the price surprise function with adaptive expectations. In terms of the quit rate he suggests that a worker will quit less frequently than real conditions warrant during inflationary times, because he knows immediately when his own wages rise, but discovers only after some time that the wage rates of others have risen. However this receives little empirical support, unlike a second hypothesis that the probability of getting a job, as measured by the vacancy rate, has a strong impact upon quits.

Thus, in general, the empirical evidence is favourable to search theories. However, as was mentioned earlier, there remains a certain degree of reticence amongst economists in accepting the validity or usefulness of this approach. Lipsey (1978) has several reservations which are probably felt more generally. First, in most models all unemployment is treated as voluntary unemployment. Secondly, as in Friedman's model, variations in the unemployment rate only occur because someone is being fooled, or lacks all the relevant information. Further criticisms are that all unemployment is regarded as search unemployment and that such models typically exclude on the job search. These last two points are relatively unimportant: the latter simply requires a fairly straightforward modification to the theories while the former simply requires us to recognise that there are other reasons for becoming unemployed than voluntary quits. Search theories have little relevance in explaining unemployment caused by a lack of demand for the product the unemployed worker's previous firm produced. But they can help to explain that person's behaviour upon becoming unemployed. The first criticism is more serious. However, Lucas (1978) has recently criticised the whole concept of voluntary unemployment. He argues that a worker who loses a good job in prosperous times does not volunteer to be in this position. Nevertheless the worker can always find some job at once. That he does not generally do so is not difficult to understand given the quality of the jobs that are easiest to find.

Thus there is an involuntary element in all unemployment, in the sense that no one chooses bad luck over good. There is equally a voluntary element in all unemployment, in the sense that however miserable one's current work options one can always choose to accept them. On the whole I agree with Lucas here. One might wish to retain the concept of voluntary unemployment to cover those who voluntarily quit their job. But even here I think the description misleading and better dropped. For, as we shall argue later, the duration of search will typically vary with labour market conditions. Thus in a boom a worker can expect to find a job with similar characteristics much more quickly than in a recession. This extra time spent searching should not, I believe, be regarded as voluntary.

The remaining point, that variations in unemployment only occur because someone is being fooled, stems from one vital assumption, that search productivity is constant. Thus in each period of search there is typically one interview regardless of economic conditions. This assumption, it should be noted, was not in Phelps. He quite explicitly noted that a higher vacancy rate will increase the probability that any unemployed person in contacting a firm will find a job open. However, Phelps's successors, driven by the need to state the individual's maximisation problem more clearly than Phelps had, made this simplifying assumption which has rarely been dropped, a notable exception to this being the paper by Parsons (1973) who, as we have already seen, links the quit decision to the probability of getting a job offer which he proxies by the vacancy rate. However, this remains an exception, which is obviously unsatisfactory as during a recession job interviews clearly decline and we can expect search productivity, defined in terms of the number of job interviews obtained in a given period, to decline too. It is this assumption which, I believe, has held back the development of search theories, limiting their explanatory power and appeal, particularly with respect to unemployment and inflation. None the less it is also my view that the search theoretic approach can and has yielded valuable insights into the inflationary process, and it is one we shall be developing in the following chapter.

Implicit Contract Theories

We turn now to examine implicit contract theory. This shares some similarities with search theories. Both have evolved from a need to explain the existence of unemployment within a market clearing framework. Both answer the question why wages do not fall enough to clear the market when there is excess supply. However, whereas search theory concentrates on aspects of labour turnover, implicit contract theory is aimed more directly at explaining layoffs.

One of the earliest and most important papers in implicit contract theory was by Baily (1974). In this he argues that firms and their owners, with their greater wealth and expertise, are better able to bear risks than workers, and thus there is an opportunity for trade. In deciding what wage–employment strategy to set the firm will be willing to reduce worker risk in return for a lower average wage. The worker, in turn, will be prepared to accept the lower wage in return for greater income security. Thus for the firm, risk reducing policies represent the most profitable way of attracting any given workforce. There are two ways in which the firm can reduce uncertainty for the worker: it can reduce either employment variations or wage variations. Both of these will reduce variations in income, but the effects are not symmetrical, because when a worker is laid off he receives a non-zero income. Thus, for layoffs the gain to the firm outweighs the loss to the worker, whereas a reduction in wages causes equal gains and losses. These alternative sources of income are from unemployment compensation, from working outside the sector considered and from the income equivalent of avoiding the disutility of work. This asymmetry may outweigh the asymmetry in the capital market. The saving from employment variations to the firm, in the form of reduced wage bills, will then outweigh the costs in the form of the higher wages the firm will have to pay. This will not be the case for wage variations, where there is no asymmetry to counter the fact that the firm is more able to bear risks, and we should expect wages to be considerably more sticky than employment.

Following a similar approach to Baily, Azariadis (1975) concludes that layoffs will be more unlikely when there is small variability in product price, above average economy wide labour demand, risk averse workers, small unemployment insurance and a highly competitive product market. The relevance of most of these is fairly obvious, with the possible exception of price stability. This is important, as if there are severe fluctuations, then in some states of the economy the costs of maintaining full employment may be very large.

Baily's paper has been criticised by Feldstein (1976) on the grounds that the logic of his argument requires that firms stabilise real wages, where the evidence is that it is money wages which are slow to adjust. In addition, he argues that employees can in fact use assets to smooth out income variations, thus questioning Baily's capital market asymmetry assumption. The analysis concerning layoffs, however, remains similar. He argues that in a competitive labour market employers will have to offer the feasible combination of unemployment, wages and conditions that workers prefer. As before, the employee will be willing to trade off spells of unemployment against a higher wage. Such trade can again take place because of the asymmetric nature of costs and benefits to employer and employee of layoffs. Feldstein concentrates on the effects of unemployment insurance, emphasising the fact that their tax exempt nature and imperfect experience rating provide the incentive for firms to lay off workers. Experience rating is a system of financing unemployment insurance unique to the United States. The insurance system is financed by the firm, whose contributions are linked to its history of generating unemployment in as much that firms whose employees draw more benefits pay higher contributions. The imperfect nature of the system arises because firms do not, in general, pay the full benefit cost of an additional layoff. This then gives added incentive to firms to lay off workers. The analysis is also relevant to other countries, such as the UK, where the benefits are financed out of an overall social security system and the marginal contribution of an extra layoff to the employer is zero.

Another early contribution in this field was by Okun (1975). He argued that the firm would attempt to appear to be a fair employer. Thus, when faced with a choice between laying off workers or reducing their wages, one argument against the latter is that it could be accused of taking advantage of the worker. In the former case this cannot be so as, although the worker gets no wages, neither does the employer receive any services from him. With respect to wages, he discusses three different types of fairness, in comparing them with the wages other employers pay, the firm's product price and consumer prices. The latter is relevant as presumably one of the advantages of a career job is the prospect of a reasonably secure and rising standard of living. Hence here Okun is quite clearly referring to maintaining, or even increasing, real wages and not just money wages.

It is interesting to note the similarity between what Okun is saying here and what Hicks (1963) was saying in *The Theory of Wages*, which was first published in 1932. In Chapter 3 he argued that firms will not cut labour at the first onset of a recession as there will be various disadvantages in doing so. It will, for example, give the firm a bad name and sour industrial relations. Therefore only when it is obvious that the recession will last will wages in general begin falling. In the following chapter he spoke of the importance of 'fair' wages, arguing that demand for a rise in wages comes in the first place because it appears fair. Finally in Chapter 7 he argued that when a man takes on a job in a regular trade he generally begins to form habits of life and expenditure which are really based on the half-conscious assumption that he will continue in that same employment more or less indefinitely. He has no legal guarantee that this will be the case, but it is not in the least surprising that he feels himself, with the flow of time, to have acquired a customary right to continue in that employment on much the same terms. If, after a time, his employer desires to reduce his wages, he feels not only that his interests have been damaged, which is certainly true, but also that he has been cheated of a legitimate expectation. The same thing is likely to happen if, instead of reducing wages, an employer merely refuses a demand for an advance made on the grounds of fairness.

Hicks tended to confine his analysis to that of a single industry or firm, rather than extending it to the labour market as a whole. But it is obvious, especially as at other times we can find hints of a search theory, that he had formulated in embryo form the basis of a modern theory of the labour market. The tragedy is that this was never developed.

More recently Akerlof (1980) has approached the concept of fair wages from rather a different angle. In building up a theory of social custom he introduces into the individual's utility function that individual's reputation in the community and the direct effects on his utility of his obedience or disobedience to the community's code of behaviour. If he believes in the code, breaking it will directly reduce his utility; if he does not believe in it there will be no such direct effect. Akerlof then argues that the question as to which customs will be obeyed is partly determined by his model and partly by history. A custom which is too costly to follow will disappear. A custom that is fairly costless to follow will, once established, continue to be followed because persons lose utility directly by disobeying the underlying social code and indirectly through their loss of reputation. Applying this to the phenomena of unemployment and wage stickiness he argues that the concept of a fair wage qualifies as a social custom for both employees and employers. If it is broken then the individual will both lose reputation and suffer a direct utility loss if he believes in the custom. None the less as a custom it will be broken if the gains outweigh these losses. For an employer these gains consist of the increased profits he gets from paying a reduced wage. For the unemployed worker the gains consist of the income he will get from having a job. It should be noted that the utility loss for an individual who does not accept the code will be less than that for an individual who does accept it. Thus we may have a situation where the custom is adhered to by a majority, but not all, of the community, with those individuals who do not accept the code offering to work for lower wages than the fair wage.

It is too soon yet to see exactly how Akerlof's theory can be integrated with explicit contract or other labour market theories. What is clear, however, is the potential importance of the theory. Indeed it may be that, as with search and implicit contract theories, it becomes one of the growth areas of economics, adding greatly to our understanding of many diverse economic phenomena.

Turning to other aspects of contract theory Grossman (1978) has examined the possibility that workers may 'break the contract' by quitting at the prospect of short-term gains, when the state of the cycle is such that their contribution to output is high. The employer then differentiates between reliable and unreliable workers by seniority, which in turn is based largely on length of service. Only senior workers will then receive insurance against income variations, while less reliable workers will be liable to spells of unemployment during which they receive little or no income. This, it is claimed, explains why employers typically do not reduce wages for those workers who are not laid off, yet pay little, if anything, to those who are. It also explains how the employer decides which workers to lay off, which previous theories did not. However, one further implication of the theory is not so in accord with reality. Workers who are not insured will need an income premium vis-à-vis what they would be prepared to accept with employment assured. Therefore, other things being equal, they should be receiving higher incomes than more reliable and hence more senior workers.

Other recent work, like Feldstein's, has tended to be somewhat critical of the early work done in this area. Phelps (1977) finds that the concept of a fixed wage solution over the life of the contract takes some getting used to. He questions some of the simplifying assumptions made in this early work, finding particularly dubious that of total worker immobility over the life of the implicit contract, according to which laid off workers do not attempt to find alternative employment. A further critical assumption concerns the worker's trust that the firm will honour the contract. The idea of a contract implies that the employer guarantees to pay a constant wage over the cycle. This then implies that he must for each state or set of circumstances employ the same numbers as he would in the absence of such a guarantee. It is here that the problem arises for how is the individual worker to know that the employer is keeping to the employment side of the contract rather than setting different employment levels based on an optimisation calculation with constant wage levels. If the worker cannot see that the firm's state or set of circumstances requires the number of lay-offs the firm claims is necessary he may distrust a contract expressed in terms of such unidentifiable states. Thus this introduces two further concepts to the problem, asymmetry in information between employer and employee and the possible gains from cheating which are open to the employer as a result of this asymmetry. Because of this Phelps argues that it may be optimal to link wages to employment, a variable clearly identifiable by all parties to the agreement. Calvo and Phelps (1977) examine some employment contingent contracts, one of their principal results being that the real wage should not be constant but vary inversely with the firm's unemployment rate. This is of course in direct contrast to the early theories on contract theory and is based on the belief that the firm will hire a worker with greater probability, and hence the lower will be the probability of being laid off, the lower the real wage.

Akerlof and Miyazaki (1980) argue that implicit contracts, even with sticky wages, will generally lead to full employment rather than layoffs. The basis for this argument is that a risk averse employee, given a choice between a wage w_1 with probability p, which represents the probability of being employed, or a zero wage with a probability of $1 - p$ and a wage $w_2 = pw_1$, will choose the latter. The firm will be indifferent to the employment guaranteeing contract and the layoff contract since the wage bill will be the same in both cases. Hence there is a possibility for a deal to be struck with the firm guaranteeing full employment and the worker accepting a lower real wage in return for this guarantee – this result again being in contradiction to the conclusions of Baily, Azariadis, etc.

Hall and Lilien (1979) are further concerned with some of the points raised by the earlier papers, although as they are most directly concerned with union–employer agreements their paper belongs more correctly in the field of explicit contracts. They are particularly concerned with four aspects of this bargaining process which they find somewhat puzzling: first, why collective bargaining agreements are rarely contingent on outside events; secondly, why employers are permitted such wide discretion in determining the level of employment when demand shifts unexpectedly; thirdly, why contracts are periodically renegotiated, and finally why in these renegotiations the current state of demand has such little impact on the new wage schedules. Their answer to the first of these is, as Phelps suggested, related to the existence of moral hazard and the difficulty in measuring these outside contingencies. Any inequalities which arise during the life of the contract can be adjusted for in periodic renegotiation of the contracts, which provides the answer to their third question, while employment contingent contracts provide a complete mechanism for taking account of unexpected shifts in demand. Finally they argue that the compensation rule specified in the contract makes workers indifferent to alternative levels of employment so that there is little or no disagreement with management's choice.

There are several points to note in connection with this paper. First, as with the paper by Phelps we have a situation where the optimal contract links the real wage to the level of employment. They show that such a compensation rule will be superior to a rule which guarantees a constant wage over the life of the contract. They then go on to consider different types of contracts under different conditions of uncertain demand, which will affect the employer's optimum strategy, and uncertain supply conditions, which affect the union's optimum strategy. They conclude that when both are uncertain an ideal, in the sense of satisfying the marginal equivalencies, employment contingent contract rule does not exist, but that it does exist when uncertainty is confined to just one of these two possibilities. For example, suppose that there are no uncertainties regarding supply conditions, an optimal contract will then equate the marginal cost of labour with labour's marginal opportunity cost, that is, set

$$B'(L) = V'(L) \qquad (1.10)$$

Integrating gives us the actual compensation rule

$$B(L) = B_0 + V(L) \qquad (1.11)$$

where $B(L)$ represents the total wage bill, $V(L)$ the union's opportunity cost of supplying the amount of labour L, and B_0 a fixed cash payment to labour which is independent of the amount of work and is chosen by the negotiators in the light of purely distributional considerations. The well-being of the union is then

$$B(L) - V(L) = B_0 + V(L) - V(L)$$
$$= B_0 \qquad (1.12)$$

which is a constant independent of L. The union never disagrees with management about L because it is indifferent among all levels of employment. Rather than a guaranteed annual wage the union has a guaranteed level of well-being.

They then go on to analyse what they call 'approximately efficient contracts', which are relevant when both demand and supply are uncertain and ideal employment contingent compensation rules do not exist. They argue that the most severe shifts will be on the demand side. It will therefore be approximately efficient for the bargainers to act as if supply side conditions were known with certainty and set the wage conditionally upon the level of employment as in (1.11).

Thus we can see that implicit contract theory is in a state of some flux. Within a few years grave doubt has been cast on the early consensus view that the theory can adequately explain sticky wages and layoff unemployment. However, before we accept these more recent analyses consideration should be given to certain weaknesses in their arguments. Take, for example, Hall and Lilien; their basic assumption is that the union's utility function is based solely on the wage bill. As we shall see later most labour economists would dispute this and argue that this utility function, if it exists at all, is much more complex. This has important implications for the more general validity of their results. Indeed, as the paper is directly concerned with explicit contracts there seem to be no clear implications for implicit contract theory at all, which, in general, is concerned with the relationship between individual workers and employers. For the individual the possible employment levels can often be narrowed down to just two, full employment or zero employment, that is, a layoff. The possibility that L could equal zero is just not considered by Hall and Lilien. Moreover the special nature of the union's objective or utility function casts doubt on the paper's relevance to explicit contract theory as well.

Turning to Akerlof and Miyazaki, a crucial assumption in their work is that workers' preferences are represented by a von Neumann–Morgenstern utility function defined on non-negative wage rates w, which is assumed to be strictly concave with a zero wage giving zero utility. However this assumption it is easy to prove the results they obtained. However the assumption that $U(0) = 0$ is unlikely to be a valid one. A zero wage implies that the worker is laid off; he will then gain utility from any non-wage income he may receive, such as unemployment insurance, as well as from the increased leisure he now enjoys. Moreover the individual will not accept employment at any wage less than w^*, where $U(w^*) = u(0)$, that is, the utility derived from this real wage must at least equal the utility from not working. Thus between a zero wage and w^* the utility function will be a horizontal line. Therefore the strict concavity assumption is also invalid and the standard von Neumann–Morgenstern analysis can no longer be used. Akerlof and Miyazaki later recognise this limitation and consider what happens when the assumption is relaxed. They argue that layoffs may then take place, but only if the worker values leisure with unemployment compensation more highly than working for a wage rate lower than w^*. However, once more this conclusion seems to be based on faulty reasoning. They argue that for layoffs to occur in a given state the firm's profits must be greater in that state if it lays off workers compared with if it employs the whole labour force, and this will be so regardless of the fact that in the second case, where employment is guaranteed, workers would accept a lower wage in return for that guarantee. In other words, if in this state the gains from having to pay fewer workers outweigh the gains from paying lower wage rates, then layoffs will take place. But this is wrong; in an implicit contract situation the employer will consider what happens over all possible states, not just one in isolation. Thus, if on average over all possible states the firm's expected profits will be greater if it does not guarantee employment compared with if it does at some lower wage acceptable to the worker, then layoffs will be a possibility over the period of the contract.

Therefore their conclusions, including a further one that the amount of unemployment generated by implicit contracts will be less than that which would be generated in a Walrasian market clearing framework, are open to doubt. Yet surprisingly enough they turn out to be valid. Layoff contingencies within a contract must have been inherited from the pre-contract, free market situation. To the extent that these can be insured against it is clear that unemployment in an implicit contract regime can be no more, and may be less, than in the absence of contracts. Moreover unemployment only occurs in the latter case if workers are unwilling to work at a market clearing wage rate, thus this must also be the reason for any unemployment possibilities within a contract.

The implicit contract literature has grown up partly to explain sticky wages within a Walrasian market clearing framework. In answer to the question why workers who have been laid off do not offer their services at a lower wage, it is suggested that sticky wages prevail due to the existence of a long-term contract between employer and employee, part of which guarantees to minimise wage variations. There may also be an incentive to reduce employment variations, but the possibility of layoffs may be an agreed part of the contract. Because of this, layoffs too have been regarded as voluntary unemployment. Another element in the growth of this literature is that it separates wage movements from current economic conditions, thus explaining the absence of a strong Phillips curve relationship in the 1970s, although it cannot explain why there should have been a relationship prior to that, nor why it should have changed in such a relatively short space of time.

The more recent contributions to the literature have been more concerned with the exact details of the contracts and have explored the possibility of contracts contingent on outside variables and upon employment. Many have come to opposite conclusions to those of early contributors in this field. However, as we have seen much of this work is open to criticism, and it is somewhat unclear in which direction the consensus will eventually move. None the less it is clear that this represents one of the most important developments in recent times and has already provided useful insights into the workings of the labour market. In my opinion the most valuable of these insights probably comes from Feldstein's and

Okun's general approach, the possibility that the employer when considering laying off workers or reducing wages in a recession will take into
account not only the immediate costs and benefits, but possible long-term
ones as well. These take the form of an expected wage premium in the
future when hiring or attempting to retain labour due to the knowledge
that he is not prepared to maintain income levels. However, valuable as
these insights are, implicit contract theories can never provide a complete
explanation of labour market phenomena, but need to be integrated with
other theories. For example, search theories can be used to explain the
proportion of laid-off workers who find alternative employment. It should
also be noted that there will be feedback from this proportion to the layoff decision, including the optimal (from the employer's point of view)
duration for layoffs. Little of this has yet been done. The theory may also
be extended to explain why employers might be reluctant to take on extra
labour in a boom, and why a firm may have several classes of worker,
skilled, unskilled, white collar, blue collar, staff and non-staff, etc. The
employer will then find it optimal to reduce uncertainty for only certain
classes of labour and to differing degrees.

Empirical work on contract theory has been limited, and what has been
done relates almost solely to the USA. One major study by Feldstein
(1978) concentrated on estimating the effect of unemployment insurance
on layoff decisions in the USA. Using regression techniques he found that
a 1 per cent increase in the ratio of potential benefits to after tax wages
increased the layoff probability for a worker by 0.7 per cent. The study
was based on the March 1971 sample of the Current Population Survey,
and in view of the fact that the mean layoff rate was 1.6 per cent, this
implies an increase in the layoff rate of about a half, a result that is difficult to believe. One possible reason for this may be the argument in the
earlier Feldstein paper that it is not the level of unemployment insurance
per se which is relevant, but rather the extent to which it is financed by
firms.

Other work has concentrated on establishing the importance of temporary layoffs. Feldstein (1976) argued that over the previous decade
there had been approximately 1.33 layoffs per 100 manufacturing employees. During the same period, there were approximately 1.11 recalls per 100
employees. He therefore concluded that at least 75 per cent of layoffs end
in recall. However, Lilien (1980) has argued that these estimates are biased
upwards, as this measure of rehires includes not only recalls from layoffs,
but also inter-establishment employee transfers. Lilien, himself, concludes
that on average 68 per cent of workers who are laid off return to their
previous employment. Furthermore, this percentage is considerably less

during recessions. Even so, many workers remain attached to the same firm through several spells of unemployment. Further, indirect support for the theory comes from Hall (1980) who notes that half of all wokers in the USA are in jobs that will last fifteen years or more. Long-term employment, of course, is a necessary, although not sufficient, condition for the validity of contract theories. Less satisfactory, however, is the fact that at any one time temporary layoffs form only a small proportion of the totally unemployed. Thus, in 1977 only 12 per cent of those unemployed were on layoff, 3 per cent temporarily so, that is, expect to be recalled within thirty days, and 9 per cent indefinitely so. This compares with 33 per cent who had lost their previous job and 13 per cent who had quit. These figures contrast sharply with those in Topel and Welch (1980). They show that in the years 1973–6 those on temporary layoff averaged 34.3 per cent of the unemployed. Apart from the different periods, the other main difference between these two sets of figures is that the former cover all the unemployed, whereas the latter relate to the unemployed in manufacturing alone. Further work by Clark and Summers (1979) suggests that temporary layoffs are also more common amongst males between the ages of 25 and 59, than amongst the rest of the population. In 1976 they estimated the proportion of the unemployed on temporary layoff, for these two groups, to be 25 per cent and 13 per cent, respectively. Furthermore they also estimate that probably no more than 50 per cent return to their previous jobs, considerably less than the other two estimates. Combining these together it would seem that temporary layoffs are most common amongst male workers in manufacturing. But, for other workers they are relatively unimportant.

An Empirical Problem

Before turning to bargaining theories we shall briefly consider a major, although unrealised, problem facing applied economists using quarterly time series data when testing theories of inflation. In general when proxying the quarterly rate of wage inflation two measures have been used. The first is the annual rate of change, centred on the month in question, which we shall denote by $\hat{W}_t$. The second is simply the quarterly rate of change itself, which we shall denote by $\dot{W}_t$. The chief advantage of the first of these two measures over the second is that it is much less volatile. In the terminology of Parkin, Sumner and Ward (1976), the use of $\hat{W}_t$ reduces the noise-to-signal ratio. The chief disadvantage is that the signal tends to get muted in the process. For example, if the underlying trend has distinct peaks and troughs these will be truncated by an annual measure of inflation.

A further consideration is the nature of the residual term relating to each of these measures. Surprisingly enough this has received relatively little attention in the literature. Some discussion can be found in Wallis (1971), who argues that the type of differencing procedure employed in the annual measure induces negative fourth order serial correlation, the reason being that a high value for W_{t+2} will lead to a high value for $\hat{W}_t$, but in four time periods a low one for $\hat{W}_{t+4}$. Implicit in this argument is the assumption that the residuals properly relate to the wage level. Rowley and Wilton (1973, 1974) argue, however, that the disturbance term relates to the 'underlying quarterly rate of inflation', in which case the residuals can be regarded as following a fourth order moving average process. Explicit in their analysis is the assumption that the same group of workers receive an increase in their wages once a year, less explicit is the assumption that this operates so that one quarter of all workers receive an increase in each quarter.

I believe that neither of these analyses, nor the conclusions associated with them, is entirely valid. We shall now expand upon this within the context of Wallis's approach. Basically I question the assumption that the residuals are serially independent. The existence of this disturbance term can be justified on several grounds, one of the most important being the variation in the number of people who receive increases in a given time period. Thus, in times of inflation, if a large number of people receive wage increases in a quarter we might expect the wage rate to be higher than would otherwise be the case. Similarly if relatively few workers receive wage increases in a quarter then we would expect a negative residual. If we now assume that each worker receives an increase once a year, then a relatively large number of increases in any one quarter will tend to be followed by a low number of increases in the succeeding three quarters.

A large number of wage increases in $t + 2$ will tend to result in a higher measure for $\hat{W}_t$ than would otherwise be expected; in other words, there will be a positive residual. This may well carry over into the following period with a further positive residual for $\hat{W}$ in $t + 1$. However, by period $t + 2$, and even more so by period $t + 3$, we might expect this to have diminished, and it is even possible that the fact that relatively few workers are receiving wage increases may result in negative second and third order serial correlation — this, in addition to the negative fourth order term noted by Wallis. However, there are other factors to consider. Individual workers in any one period may receive wage increases in excess of, or less than, what would be expected given the underlying economic conditions. This will cause the wage index to lie above its trend level until the following year, when their wages are renegotiated, and will result in positive first, second and third order serial correlation. The overall pattern in the disturbance term will then be the result of the sum of these two effects.

Thus, in comparing these conclusions with those of Wallis's it can be seen that they differ in as much as we suggest the existence of a much more complex disturbance term than he thought likely. While regarding the work of Rowley and Wilton, I believe their assumption that the same number of workers receive an increase in each quarter to be much too rigid. Indeed I believe that this invalidates much of their empirical analysis. This interest in the residuals of $\hat{W}_t$ has not been extended to the purely quarterly measure of the inflation rate, $\dot{W}_t$, apart from Parkin, Sumner and Ward's comment that this appears to be a very noisy series. However, it seems unlikely that this is pure white noise, as has been assumed hitherto. The key lies with the observation already made, that a large number of increases in any one quarter will lead to a small number in the following three periods. This implies the existence of negative first, second and third order serial correlation.

Wage Bargaining Theories

A completely different approach to inflation, which to some extent predates the excess demand approach, is to view wage determination as the outcome of a bargaining process, between employers on the one side and trade union leaders on the other. Within this approach there are several different strands of development, not all of which we shall be concerned with here. For example, we shall not be examining the key sector hypothesis. Nor shall we be concerned with models that postulate that the principal thrust of union policy is to establish and maintain a certain differential over non-union wages, or to be involved in a fight over income shares. It may well be that, as a result of unions' actions, a union/non-union differential is established. It may also be, again as a result of unions' actions, that the share of labour's income in the national cake increases over time. But it does not seem to me that these are the result of intentional planning as much as a consequence of unions' actions in maintaining their memberships' standard of living. Thus, explanations of inflation couched in terms of unions attempting to increase either the union/non-union differential or the share of wages in national income seem to me to be ill-conceived. We shall therefore be examining these theories only when they have some relevance to the more general problem.

A relatively early formulation of a bargaining theory can be found in Hansen (1921), who observed that, for the period 1900–20, strike activity tended to increase in prosperous years. He explained this by arguing that at such times prices and living costs rise which leads to demands for money wage increases. Profits also increase and this, he suggested, would give rise to a conflict over their distribution. Thus, already we have mentioned two variables which were to become the mainstay of many subsequent theories of wage bargaining. One further interesting point is that in the two decades that preceded the turn of the century, when economic activity was in a long period of decline, strikes were negatively correlated with the price level. Hansen suggested that this may be due to cyclical downturns sparking off defensive strikes.

Another early study, first published in 1928, by Hiller (1969) suggested that the timing of strikes might be determined by tactical advantage. He argued that in prosperous times unions were more liable to launch agressive strikes due to employer vulnerability stemming from their unwillingness to sacrifice high profits and the scarcity of strike breakers. Also important were the fact that wage increases could be passed on to consumers and the relatively strong position of workers and unions. When the economy is in decline most strikes are defensive, with workers attempting to maintain their existing wages.

One of the earliest theories, it was first published in 1932, to pay attention to the bargaining process itself was developed by Hicks (1963). As with much of the literature on bargaining, he was partially concerned with explaining the occurrence of strikes. He constructed a schedule of wages and lengths of strike, setting opposite each period of stoppage the highest wage an employer would be willing to concede rather than endure a stoppage of that duration. At this wage the expected cost of the stoppage and the expected cost of concession just balance. He called this the employer's concession schedule. Similarly he constructed a resistance curve giving the length of time for which the employees would be willing to strike rather than allow their remuneration to fall below the corresponding wage. He then argues that the point where these two curves intersect, point A in Figure 1.2, will represent the highest wage that can be extracted from the employer. Indeed, if both parties know the shape of the other's schedule with certainty this will be the wage that is agreed upon. Industrial disputes can then only occur if one of the two parties wrongly estimate the other's schedule, for example, if the employer believes the union's schedule to lie to the left of where it actually is, or unions believe the employer's curve lies above where it actually is. Strikes are therefore the product of imperfect information.

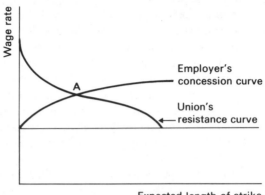

Figure 1.2   *Concession and resistance curves in Hicks's model*

Hicks then argues that the actual wage level arrived at will depend upon the position of the two curves. For the union, of critical importance is their ability to withstand a strike. This depends upon the size of the union strike fund, the savings of the membership, the willingness of other unions to help and of shopkeepers to give credit. The greater the extent of such resources, the stronger the union will be, and the more likely it will be able to secure a given level of wages. The position of the employer's concession curve will depend upon three factors which are in fact interrelated: first, the degree to which the union can make the strike effective in causing a stoppage of the employer's business; secondly, the direct costs of the stoppage, that is, revenue forgone; and thirdly the indirect losses through breaking of contracts and disappointment of customers.

Two years before Hicks's study was published, Zeuthan (1930) also directly analysed the bargaining process in a book, which, like Hicks's, has had a considerable impact right through to the present day. He modelled bargaining as a process by which both sides continually make concessions until agreement is reached. It is assumed that both sides are pessimistic about the outcome of a possible strike. Thus although there are gains from negotiating for an improved settlement to both sides, there are also potential costs in the risk of a strike that will result from failure to agree. It is therefore in the interests of both parties to move towards the other's position, as this will lower the other side's benefits from disagreement relative to its costs. Either side will stop conceding when a concession would give it a smaller relative gain than it believes the other side to be securing.

More explicitly let U_{ij} represent the utility to i of j's offer. Thus, for example, U_{uu} represents the utility for the union from its own offer and U_{ue} from the employer's offer. Let r_u and r_e represent the probability of a strike as perceived by the union and employer, respectively. In the event of a strike the union believes a low wage will result and attaches a utility of S_u to this outcome. The employer is also pessimistic and believes a high wage will result, which will yield a utility of S_e. The union will be willing to risk conflict as long as the gains of doing so outweigh the costs. The critical point will be when they are equal, that is,

$$r_u(U_{ue} - S_u) = (1 - r_u)(U_{uu} - U_{ue}) \qquad (1.13)$$

The left-hand side represents the expected cost of rejecting the employer's offer. It equals the probability, or risk, of a strike multiplied by the reduced utility of the wage expected to be negotiated after the strike compared with the employer's current offer. The right-hand side measures the expected gains of rejecting the employer's current offer. It equals the probability of the employer agreeing to the union's demand without a strike multiplied by the increased utility of that wage compared with the employer's current offer. A similar condition can be derived for the employer.

From these expressions further ones can be derived giving the maximum risk of a strike that each side is willing to face in pressing for a wage claim different from what the other side has offered; for example,

$$r_u = \frac{U_{uu} - U_{ue}}{U_{uu} - S_u} \qquad (1.14)$$

and similarly for the employer.

Zeuthan then suggests that the side with the lower maximum acceptable risk will be the one to make the concession, in an attempt to reduce for the other side the gains of a strike, as their determination to withstand a strike is the greater. If both sides' maximum risks are equal then both will make concessions in order to avoid deadlock. If, however, this is not the case, and it is the union who makes the concession in the form of a reduction in its demand, this will have the effect of increasing U_{eu}, the utility to the employer of that offer. This in turn will lower r_e, the maximum strike risk he is prepared to accept, and it will also reduce r_u, but not by as much. Then, provided the union's concession has been great enough, the employer will now be the one least prepared to risk a strike and he will make the next concession by increasing his wage offer. Provided there is perfect information this process will continue until agreement is reached. This agreement will, in the symmetric case Zeuthan assumed, result in an equal division of gains from bargaining compared to the utilities they could have expected to have derived in the event of a strike.

It has been suggested by Harsanyi (1956) that Zeuthan's solution is mathematically equivalent to Nash's (1950, 1953) solution, which was based on game theory. The basis of Nash's argument is that if both sides' utilities are measured by von Neumann–Morgenstern cardinal utility functions, agreement will be reached at the point where the product of utility gains compared with the conflict situation is maximised. It is easy to see that in the symmetric case this solution too will give equal shares to both sides; hence in this particular case it is equivalent to the Zeuthan example.

Perhaps the most interesting element in Nash's theory, from our current point of view, occurs when he considers non-co-operative threat games, where each side has a choice amongst alternative threats that it can use to bring pressure upon the other side. He analyses the problem of choosing an optimal threat under the assumption that bluffing is not allowed, that is, threats when made have to be followed through. Harsanyi shows that an optimal threat may increase the cost to oneself provided that it increases the cost to one's opponent in a greater proportion. If either side were to put forward a threat which in the event of conflict implied a disproportionate burden to itself then the other side would know it was bluffing.

The joint property of the Zeuthan and Nash models has come to be known as the 'split the difference' theory of wage bargaining. Hamermesh (1973) has tested this theory using data relating to forty-three negotiations in the USA concluded between September 1968 and December 1970. He found that the final settlement lay much nearer to the employer's initial offer than to the union's initial demand, thereby implying that either the two parties' utility functions are not identical or linear with respect to wage increases, or that unions bluff more than employers, or that the split the difference theory is inapplicable. Bowlby and Schriver (1978), in a similar study, use data from the Tennessee Valley Authority which are available in greater detail and over a longer time period than the Hamermesh data. On the basis of this they conclude that unions do bluff more than employers, the reasons being sociological and political rather than economic. However, they also highlight the difficulty of testing the Zeuthan–Nash theory which for a full test would require data on wages that both sides would be willing to settle for at each stage of the bargaining process. This of course is not available.

Political factors have also received emphasis in Ross (1948). He views unions as essentially political organisations; union wage policy is then determined by the pressures acting on the union leadership. Union leaders will try and reconcile the various pressures, attempting to achieve a compromise between them, rather than attempting to maximise wages, employment or some combination of the two. The main pressures are internal, arising from the different groupings that constitute the membership. Other pressures come from other levels of the union, other unions or the government. In reconciling the various pressures the leaders have considerable range of choice in formulating wage demands due to the membership's dependence on their guidance. But none the less they must ultimately satisfy the membership as their survival and perhaps that of the unions depends on it.

Ross's views brought an immediate retort from Dunlop (1950) who rejected his analysis mainly on the grounds that in the long run economic factors will determine wage/employment combinations. Union leaders, he argued, know and act in accordance with the economic facts of life. He suggested a model by which unions maximise their membership with respect to a wage membership function. More specifically he suggested that unions should be considered as aiming to set a wage which maximises the wage bill, or alternatively which ensures that only union members are employed. These two papers set the tone for a continuing debate on whether union behaviour should be analysed primarily within an economic or a political context. Each thought that both factors were relevant, but whereas Ross chose to emphasise the political factors, Dunlop thought that in the long run economic factors would override these.

Within the spirit of Dunlop's views is the analysis by Eckstein and Wilson (1962). They examine the variables, both labour and product market ones, which influence the costs of settlements and strikes to the bargaining participants. Thus, on the trade union side members expect large settlements in good times and make it difficult for union leaders to settle for less. Similarly, for employers the disutility of large settlements varies with economic conditions. When demand is high and the market is considered tight firms will show little concern over loss of sales to their rivals. On the other hand, when demand is low prices cannot easily be raised and wage increases are more likely to come out of profits. Secondly, when profits are low, high wage settlements increase the risk of managements having to disappoint stockholders and generally complicate managements' financial problems. In addition they also feel that the costs of strike action and the probability of winning vary with economic conditions. Thus, in good times, when operating rates are high, the loss of profits during a strike is great. However, the hazard of losing customers to competitors may be greater when the product market is not prosperous and competition is keener. On the union side the loss of earnings is greater in prosperous times, but the employees may be better able to withstand the loss.

More recent studies in this tradition, both in the USA and the UK, have had to take cognisance of the fact that an increasing standard of living in much of the postwar era does not seem to have satisfied workers who apparently have come to expect this to continue. Partly as a consequence this work has, in some respects, become more sophisticated. Johnston (1972) and Johnston and Timbrell (1973) propose a model whereby the union makes a claim for a wage increase of amount ΔW^e. The employer's response is assumed to be determined by the principle of minimising his expected costs. Important here is the employer's assessment of the union's real claim, ΔW^{re}, which is defined as the size of the offer that has to be made in order to reduce the probability of a strike to zero. The main conclusions which emerge from their analysis are that the size of the wage settlement will be positively related to the employer's estimate of the real claim, the rate of time discounting used by the employer, the current rate of profit per unit of output or per man, the employer's estimate of δ, the union's propensity to endure a strike, and the subjective costs imposed upon the employer by the strike. It will also be negatively related to the time span over which the employer discounts.

The role of most of these variables is fairly obvious. Of special interest, however, is the employer's estimate of the real claim, which in this explicit form is largely unique to this model, although it is implied in the theory of differential bluffing we examined earlier in Hamermesh's study. There are several determinants of this, but in their analysis Johnston and Timbrell lay special emphasis upon price expectations. They argue that if unions are concerned with the real wage, then the higher they expect the rate of inflation to be, the greater will be their wage claims and the vigour with which they are pursued, thus leading a rational employer to increase his estimate of both ΔW^{re} and δ.

They also lay special emphasis upon the effects of tax changes on real income. During the postwar years the retention ratio, that is, the ratio of net to gross income, has been steadily falling for all workers. They put forward the hypothesis that unions attempt to allow for unfavourable movements in the retention ratio. Alternatively they suggest that unions have a target level of real wage growth, and if actual growth falls short of this target, whether due to changes in the tax structure, unforseen price movements or whatever, then in succeeding years they will attempt to compensate for this shortfall. This latter argument is an extremely important one and the forerunner of more recent work.

Much of the literature which we have surveyed so far has concentrated upon the variables that influence unions' demands, for example, the level of profits and the rate of unemployment. An alternative approach is concerned with measuring trade union militancy. An obvious proxy for this is some measure of strike activity, as has been used by Taylor (1970) and Godfrey (1971), for example. There are, however, obvious empirical problems in the use of such a variable, for example, what is the appropriate measure to use, the number of strikes, days lost or workers involved. In addition, should the measure be restricted to strikes over wages or should it include all strikes? But apart from these difficulties of definition, a major problem with the variable is that it lacks any firm foundation in economic theory. It has been used because it seems intuitively plausible that increased trade union militancy will be associated with an increase in strike activity. Yet is it not just as plausible to assert that increased 'employer militancy' might also be coupled with an increase in strike activity? A strike over money wages occurs because the employer makes an offer which the union finds unacceptable and no suitable compromise can be reached. It is by no means obvious that this will always be because the trade union leader is being more militant in his demands rather than the employer being more militant in his offer. Indeed if we follow Hicks's or Zeuthan's theories we should associate increased strike activity with an increase in the degree of uncertainty that surrounds collective bargaining.

An alternative measure which does not suffer from these objections has been proposed by Hines (1964). The gist of his argument is that trade union militancy is manifested in areas other than the actual wage bargaining process. Specifically he argues that unions would regard a successful membership drive as a prerequisite for success in this process. Therefore when a union puts in a wage claim it will seek immediately before and during the period of negotiation to increase its bargaining power by increasing the proportion of the labour force over which it has direct control. A measure of trade union militancy is therefore provided by the rate of change of the labour force that is unionised.

When tested empirically by Hines and others there does appear to be a significant relationship between wage inflation and this measure of militancy, both in the UK and the USA. However, this has not resulted in any general acceptance of the hypothesis by economists, and ever since it was first proposed there has been a constant battle between Hines and his many protagonists. In particular his results have been criticised on statistical grounds. But it remains true that even when all the statistical irregularities have been removed from his regressions, the change in union density has remained a significant variable within wage equations. Consequently much of the debate has centred on the interpretation that should be placed upon this significance.

Purdy and Zis (1973) argue that workers will tend to join unions as a defensive measure to secure strike benefit when a strike seems likely. If the strike leads to an increase in wages this would then explain the statistical findings. It has also been suggested that when trade unions secure wage increases, for whatever reason, the union may attract an increase in its membership. However, it seems to me that neither of these alternatives is any more convincing than Hines's original one, especially when it comes to explaining the very large increases in union membership that occurred simultaneously with the wage explosion in the UK at the beginning of the 1970s, the fact that this increase was mainly amongst white collar workers with a relatively low propensity to strike, and the fact that in the USA the wage explosion there saw no such increase in union membership.

A further criticism of this whole approach to the wage bargaining process is that the term militancy seems to be a catch-all phrase for almost anything that tends to increase wages or wage demands. One distinction which has been made, again by Purdy and Zis, is between power and militancy. Power reflects the capacity to influence the bargaining process via, for example, strike action, while militancy reflects the will to exercise such power. However, a second distinction may also be made. We have already observed that to some extent these militancy variables have been used as substitutes for other variables, such as profits and unemployment, which influence the size of the union's claim and eventual settlement wage. But this concept of militancy is not in accordance with the ordinary usage of the term. Perhaps a better practice would be to try and differentiate between unions' actions when faced with essentially the same set of economic conditions. If, in such a situation, one union pursues a wage claim in excess of that pursued by another union, then we can say that the first union is in some sense more militant than the second. If, however, the same union in one year is faced with a situation where profits are higher and unemployment lower than in a previous year, and it attempts to secure a higher wage increase than previously, is the union being more militant than before? There are also questions relating to who exactly is being militant, the leaders of the union or the membership, and what exactly is the relationship between these two groups.

It is clear that such questions are leading us back to the political view of the union advocated by Ross, which is also the starting point for one of the most important studies of recent years. Ashenfelter and Johnson (1969) begin with the assumption that there are three parties involved in labour–management negotiations: the management, the union leadership and the union rank and file. The objectives of the leadership are, first, the growth and survival of the union as an institution and, secondly, their own personal political survival. These two objectives are accomplished by satisfying the expectations of the rank and file as well as possible. From an employer's point of view they argue that a strike could perform the function of reducing the minimal wage increase that is acceptable to the rank and file.

They then go on to argue that initially this wage will depend negatively on the unemployment rate, as when this is low the typical worker has the chance of moving to a higher paid job, but he will first try and secure a wage increase from his present employer. In addition the leadership will be less likely to reduce this minimal wage aspiration when unemployment is low, because the employment effects of a large wage increase will have little effect upon their political stature, and a sizeable strike fund may replace part of the worker's lost income. Finally, there will be decreased opposition, among the rank and file, to a militant course of action since there will be part-time opportunities for potential strikers.

They then suggest that a second determinant of this wage should be a moving average of past real wage changes, weighted in accordance with an inverted U distribution, this being intended to capture the difference between the expected long-run increase in real wages and the currently anticipated increase. An increase in this difference will cause an increase in the wage acceptable to the union membership. Profits are also likely to be relevant on the grounds that if a firm's profits have been high in recent periods, the typical union member may feel that he deserves a larger wage increase. Also the motivation of the leadership to attempt the task of persuading the membership to be content with a lower settlement will be diminished.

It is then suggested that y_0, the minimum acceptable wage, will fall with a strike. The employer's problem is to maximise profits. He has the choice of agreeing to y_0 and avoiding a strike, or of rejecting y_0 and incurring a strike, which will result in a lower wage increase. In effect the firm must weigh the effect on profits of strike costs against the possibly lower wage costs that can be expected to follow a strike. For the union leader a strike performs the task of lowering his membership's expectations due to the shock effect of the firm's resistance and the resultant loss of normal income. After some time the leadership will feel that the minimum acceptable wage has fallen to an acceptably low level to enable them to safely sign the agreement with the management. Thus, in comparison with earlier bargaining models, strikes do not occur because one or other of the two sides misinterprets the other's position. Nor does a strike imply that either the union leader or the employer must be irrational. Irrationality is present in their model, but it is the workers who are ignorant of the full economic facts. The strike is then a means of educating them only to be used as a last resort.

Limited support for Ashenfelter and Johnson's theory comes from a study by Farber (1978). In testing it he uses a sample base composed of eighty wage contracts relating to ten different firms for the period 1954–70 in the USA. In his interpretation of the model he argues that the speed with which the minimum acceptable wage falls with respect to the duration of a strike will be a function of two factors. The first is the ability of the union members to replace lost income during a strike through such things as strike benefits or alternative employment opportunities. The second is the militancy or mood of the rank and file as determined by such things as previous changes in real wages and how effective they can expect a strike to be in terms of imposing costs on the employer. In the empirical work two of the variables were significant: first, a dummy variable to represent outside pressure on the union during periods of incomes policy, in effect the wage guidelines of 1962–6, and secondly, labour's share of total sales, which was hypothesised to be directly related to the ability of the union to cause a cessation of supplies in the short run.

Hibbs (1976) has also developed a model which is in some respects similar to Ashenfelter and Johnson's, at least in as much as it argues that strikes are related to disparities between actual and expected real wage changes in the recent past, where expected wage changes are formed by an extrapolative expectations model. The net effect of this is a similar distributed lag function to the one suggested by Ashenfelter and Johnson. His results indicate that an equilibrium reduction of 1 per cent in the rate of change of real wages is associated with a strike volume increase of the order of 59 man-days per 1000 workers, which is distributed nonlinearly over about five periods. But the real novelty in the paper is to be found in the theoretical discussion where he introduces concepts from social psychology. The essence of the theory is that aggressive or violent behaviour is caused in part by a gap between expectation and achievement. He quotes from Krech and Crutchfield (1948, p. 542) that 'A wage rate is psychologically inadequate, no matter how large in absolute amount, if it results in a wide discrepancy between the worker's level of aspiration and his level of achievement.'

This is similar to Runciman's (1966) notion of relative deprivation, by which when the growth of real income is low relative to expectations people come to feel relatively deprived. These expectations are determined by a person's own earlier experience, and by observations of other people's real incomes. Individuals then attempt to obtain wage increases which will bring their real wages in line with their desired real wage. Laidler and Parkin (1975) dismiss this hypothesis on the grounds that it either requires that people suffer from money illusion, or it is in all essentials equivalent to Friedman's expectations hypothesis. Unfortunately they do not expand on this criticism, which to me is far from obvious.

Indeed the concept of a catch-up variable, as it may be called, is becoming commonplace in many empirical studies of wage inflation, important examples being those of Henry, Sawyer and Smith (1976) for the UK and Perry (1978) for the USA, both of which were discussed earlier.

Reflections on Bargaining Theories

Several points have emerged from this survey of the literature. The first is the relevance of the earlier contributions even today, and how often they seem to be rediscovered. Thus by 1928 we already have a link between union aggression and the business cycle, in particular profits and product and labour market conditions. We have the suggestion that tactical considerations determine the timing of strikes. We can also find the argument that price increases will lead to demands for money wage increases, thereby implying that workers are bargaining for real wages. One of the few really new concepts to have emerged in recent years has been that of rising workers' aspirations and the effects of deviations of actual income from those expectations. The second point is that not all of these theories are necessarily mutually exclusive. Zeuthan's and Nash's theories relate to the bargaining process itself, and can be combined with other theories which have perhaps been more concerned with the determinants of each side's bargaining position.

Thirdly, it has become evident that much of the literature has been primarily concerned with explaining strikes, rather than wage inflation itself. The occurrence of a strike can only reduce the size of the cake which eventually has to be divided between the two sides. As such, either the strike represents irrational behaviour or arises out of ignorance, as in the Hicks, Zeuthan and Nash models. However, I find neither of these alternatives particularly appealing. The universal pessimism which characterises Zeuthan's model I find to be unrealistic. The hypothesis that workers only go on strike when they or their leaders are misinformed seems equally so. The facts seem to be that both workers and employers countenance strikes when the gains cannot possibly cover the costs when measured in money terms. Yet neither does the concept of people behaving irrationally appeal. One possible alternative may be that for one of the two sides the negotiation is just one of several with which it is concerned, for example, a union negotiating with several different employers, or a local authority negotiating with several different sets of workers and hence their unions. In this case the wage award in any negotiation may influence those in others. The union or employer may well then countenance a strike in the belief that the overall gains to it will outweigh the costs of that particular strike.

I feel that this may well be an important possibility and would explain many of the strikes which do occur, but it is unlikely in itself to be a complete explanation. For such an explanation we probably need to go outside the borders of economics to the political theories of Ross, and the social psychological theories of Hibbs and Runciman. Alternatively we might perhaps stay within the bounds of economic theory, but recognise that utility is also attached to employment and the status to which that employment gives rise, as well as to consumption financed by income from that employment. The level of utility associated with a particular job may itself be related to the associated income, independent of any consumption it can finance.

In recent years more attention has been paid to the consequences of bargaining theories for inflation. There are problems here, however. First, in the USA only a relatively small minority of the labour force is unionised. For trade unions and the bargaining structure associated with them to have a key role in explaining inflation, there needs to be some kind of transfer mechanism by which wage increases in the unionised sectors are generalised throughout the remainder of the economy. One possible reason for the existence of such spillover effects may be that non-union employers will not want to fall too far behind union wage rates for fear of their workforce being tempted to unionise. Some work has been done in an attempt to find evidence for such effects (Johnson, 1977; and Flanagan, 1976), but the results are inconclusive, even contradictory, with evidence in some cases for a spillover effect in the other direction. In addition economists have in general been sceptical of the theoretical arguments behind such a link.

A further problem with collective bargaining theories of inflation lies with the changed nature of the Phillips curve since 1970. There have been two approaches to explaining this change. First, that of Hines, which argues that increased militancy on the part of union leaders is the root cause of this change. This in itself, however, is not an answer; it merely changes the question to why did unions become more militant at this time. In answering this further question some economists have been drawn into seeking general sociological answers in terms of an eroding of the traditional values and attitudes in society. We shall be examining this approach shortly. Alternatively one might attribute this militancy directly to disappointed workers' aspirations, as in the relative deprivation hypothesis. This alternative lies at the heart of Henry, Sawyer and Smith's, Johnston and Timbrell's and Ashenfelter and Johnson's analyses. But it has not been properly thought through. For example, in much of the empirical work it is implied that in addition to workers wanting more when wages fall behind expectations, the reverse is also true, that is, they will tend to want less when actual wages lie above expectations. In addition, the justification, in economic terms, for continually rising aspirations is not made. This, after all, represents a considerable departure from previous theories, which assumed, if they assumed anything at all, that workers would merely attempt to maintain living standards constant over time. Increasing real wages was of course an objective, but only to be secured when economic conditions were right.

One final criticism of all these theories is that they view the employer's aim as one of negotiating as low a wage as possible, in order to minimise costs or to maximise profits. However, this ignores the insights we have gained from search and implicit contract theories, that employers will take into account the effects of the wages they pay on the ease with which they can attract and retain labour, which will in turn affect their profits or costs. It is the integration of these insights into a bargaining framework that lies at the heart of the theory that will be presented in the next chapter.

Summary and Conclusions

The survey that has been presented illustrates that economists have failed to comprehend the theoretical problems associated with the inflationary period of the 1970s. The feeling of certainty and satisfaction which followed Phillips' original article has evaporated. The consequence of this is that we can offer no cure for inflation with the certainty that it will work. Of course many economists would deny this. They would insist that they do understand the economic forces behind inflation. But their constantly changing positions, the lack of any unified approach to the problem within the profession as a whole, and the failure to achieve some measure of stability to the price level after at least a decade of trying would suggest otherwise. This is not to deny that the 1970s has seen some original and valuable insights into the workings of the labour market. But these have not combined together to give us a thorough understanding of the problem as a whole.

This failure, and failure it is, has led some economists to seek answers from other disciplines. Thus Wiles (1973) has argued that to seek a purely economic model of inflation is a mistake since this will depend upon the subjective state of mind of union leaders. The breakdown of the Phillips curve is then linked to increased union disregard for the social consequences of their actions. Williamson and Wood (1976) also find it probable that the 1970 explosion of wage inflation in the UK was caused partly by the increasing readiness of unions to inflict direct harm on the public in ways that had previously been unthinkable. Although such explanations may be uncomfortably *ad hoc* they find them at least consistent with the facts, which they argue is more than can be claimed for more aesthetically pleasing theories.

These alternative approaches are set out most forcibly in a volume edited by Hirsch and Goldthorpe (1978). Hirsch, in summarising the contributions to this volume, highlighted two distinct approaches. The first argues that the existence of an aspirations gap between workers' aspirations and their living standards is a crucial factor. Panic, in his contribution, argues that this aspirations gap is based partly on the workers' own past experience, but also partly with reference to living standards in other countries. To reduce inflation this aspirations gap needs to be closed, either by increasing the productive capacity of the economy, or by reducing aspirations. This, it is argued, must be done by both checking excessive aspirations and by reducing the extent to which individuals collectively through, for example, trade unions use force in attempting to attain those aspirations. Hirsch suggests that this corresponds, not to a failure of the market system, but of the political and institutional foundations of that system, which have developed incompatible features.

The second approach locates the fault more directly with the market economy itself. Goldthorpe, whose contribution lies within this approach, argues that over recent decades the increase in the rate of inflation has reflected a situation in which conflict between social groups has become both more intense and more equally matched. The less well-off groups within our society have become less hesitant in the pursuit of what they see as their own interests. As a consequence of this they are better able to achieve those objectives. He then specifies three factors which have led to this change.

The first of these is the decay of the status order. He argues that once this is removed there is no obvious reason why the pay claims of different workers should not expand and lead to the pursuit of relativities which are inconsistent. Secondly, there is the realisation of citizenship. By citizenship he means the extent to which all members of a nation possess in common a body of civil, political and social rights. This has led to measures which increase the rights of workers, for example, the 'right to work', or of their representatives to be involved in the decision making process of the firm. The right to work is now a normative concept, and not simply a probabilistic concept based on postwar experience. Attempts by governments to control union pushfulness by creating unemployment have therefore met much greater resistance than before in the form of sit-ins and the like. This then reduces the efficiency of such measures in combating inflation.

These two factors interrelate with a third. The decay of the status order has freed workers from inhibitions relating to notions of their social inferiority. The growth of citizenship has widened and strengthened the various forms of action open to them. But the full impact of these changes will be felt only when there has grown up a working class, aware of their identity as such, whose experience relates solely to these changed conditions. Such a working class is then described as being mature. This definition of maturity, which is somewhat different to those used previously, is satisfied in the UK, although not in the USA. In the former trade unionism is for workers the normal mode of action by which living standards are to be maintained and improved. This has then paved the way for concerted and combined union action to defend the rights of the working class as a whole, ready to countenance civil and economic disorder in this defence.

Goldthorpe admits that his analysis cannot stand alone without economic analysis. Sociological variables need to be integrated with economic ones, such as the level of demand, in a unified theory of inflation. But, none the less, the basic reason for the breakdown of the Phillips curve is the change in the social order which has given rise to more intense and more equally matched conflict than hitherto. I find, with an economist's traditional bias, little merit in this approach. One would have thought that such a process would have brought a gradual change in the inflation–unemployment relationship, not a sudden one as appears to have happened. One would also have thought that, in the UK, the most obvious example of workers joining together to defend their interests as a class was the general strike of 1926. Yet surely this was long before the emergence of a mature working class by Goldthorpe's definition. In addition, how is such an analysis to explain inflation in the USA and other countries, where workers seem to be taking their time in attaining maturity? I find more merit in Panic's approach. Indeed to an extent it parallels my own as well as that of certain other economists. But I would argue, and this is perhaps mainly semantics, that this approach can be maintained within the borders of economic theory.

This is not to deny a role to these other disciplines, but it is essentially supportive. For example, elements from psychology can help us to better understand the way people form expectations with respect to inflation and other variables. Elements from social psychology may usefully illuminate certain aspects of the bargaining process. It may also be that as aspirations are continually disappointed there is a decay in social cohesion which feeds back into the inflationary process. But I would argue that such decay is not a direct cause of inflation, but should perhaps be more correctly regarded as one of its symptoms. I believe that the essential causes of inflation are basically economic, and that, despite the failures of recent years, they can be analysed within a largely economic framework.

We shall now attempt to do this by expanding upon and combining certain elements from the literature just surveyed. Within this literature we have seen that there have been two main approaches. Until 1970 most economists accepted the excess demand approach as providing a fairly satisfactory explanation of inflation. But the apparent breakdown, or weakening, of the Phillips curve and the associated failures of governments to curb inflation by deflationary policies, have led to a ferment of new ideas. This is often the case – it is when the accepted paradigm ceases to work that the incentive to find a new one becomes greatest. It is also often the case that many of the theories which emerge from the melting pot fail to stand the test of time, and are discarded when a new, generally accepted, paradigm emerges.

Those economists who have advocated an excess demand approach to inflation have been particularly active in fostering new ideas. The most important contribution has come from those who have combined the Walrasian market clearing framework with Muth's rational expectations hypothesis. The approach can perhaps be identified as being mainly monetarist inspired, although there are exceptions. It has led to an enormous volume of often highly sophisticated literature, on such questions as government policy impotency, feedback rules from events to policies, and the cognitive problem of how people learn about the true economic model and its parameters. However, it seems to me that the foundations upon which the theory rests are unsound, and that when a new paradigm eventually emerges this theory will be mainly discarded, with perhaps some of its more acceptable manifestations, such as feedback rules, being absorbed into that paradigm.

The increased level of unemployment has, independently of any change in the Phillips curve, been exerting economists' minds, particularly those who have argued within a market clearing framework. They have essentially rejected Keynes' notion of underfull employment equilibrium, and have sought solutions which imply that this increase in unemployment reflects an increase in the natural rate, and should therefore be regarded as an increase in voluntary unemployment. This has stimulated interest in search theories, and was a major factor in the appearance of implicit contract theories. Search is often regarded as an information gathering exercise. Partly because of this, and partly because within search theories the unemployed reject wage offers in the expectation of receiving a better one, search unemployment is regarded as voluntary. This I believe to be a weakness in the theory, which will be examined in the next chapter. Implicit contract theories view workers as making a contract with an employer where the probability of being unemployed is specified. However, in making this contract the participants will take into consideration economic conditions. In certain circumstances, if a higher level of unemployment is expected to prevail in the future than previously, a rational individual may accept a higher layoff probability. But this does not imply that this is voluntary, that he wants to be laid off, or that the government should be unconcerned when he and others in a similar position are laid off. The analogy can be made between a man given the choice between execution by firing squad or by hanging. Having made the choice rationally, he can scarcely be accused of committing suicide.

Search theories in particular have been the subject of considerable, and often valid, criticism. But despite this I believe that they offer the most realistic opportunity of understanding the labour market. It is because of this that I shall be developing such a theory in the following chapter, which it is hoped will meet many of the criticisms that have been made, and remove some of the limitations. I shall then be incorporating certain aspects of implicit contract theory into it. This will then give us half of our theory of inflation. The other half will come from developing a wage bargaining theory in which employers enter negotiations with the aim of negotiating a wage which is determined by the effects of that wage on their ability to function in the labour market. This differs from other bargaining theories which argue that they attempt to negotiate as low a wage as possible.

It is the development of these two approaches and their synthesis into one general model of inflation that will occupy us in the next chapter. As a result of this synthesis I hope to be able to explain some of the phenomena which have troubled economists in the 1970s, such as the breakdown or weakening of the Phillips curve, the existence of and fluctuations in unemployment, the growth of worker or trade union militancy coupled with the growth of trade unions in the UK together with their decline in the USA. On the policy side doubts will be raised as to whether any of the standard policy measures can have any real effect on inflation where the UK is concerned, whereas for the USA I would suggest that inflation as a problem should largely disappear in the 1980s and that the government should be more concerned with unemployment. A gradual reflation of the economy would seem to be the optimal policy coupled with energy saving and oil substitution measures. Finally I shall argue against the famous and oft quoted dictum that inflation is always and everywhere a monetary phenomenon.

Chapter 2

A Synthesis

In the previous chapter we saw how there had grown up two alternative theoretical approaches to inflation, the one centred on the market clearing mechanism, the other on collective bargaining. Hitherto, these two approaches have generally been regarded as being mutually exclusive, with the acceptance of one precluding the acceptance of the other. However, it seems to me that both contain elements of the truth which the other ignores. Therefore by combining these two theories we get a more complete analysis of the inflationary process. Excess demand theories of inflation emphasise the employer's role, whereby he reacts to demand conditions in the labour market by varying the wages he pays. However, to a large extent they ignore, or at best give only a cursory analysis of, the role of trade unions. Thus, for example, both Friedman (1968) and Phelps (1968) make the assumption that the principal motivation of unions is to maintain some differential over non-union workers. The implication of this assumption is that inflation is basically determined in the non-unionised sectors, with the unionised sectors passively responding.

However, I do not believe, as I stated earlier, that this view regarding the union's role is correct. I believe, for reasons that will be expanded upon later, that the primary aim of unions is to maintain their members' standards of living. It may well be that, because workers acting collectively are better able to do this than workers acting alone, there will be some differential between organised and unorganised workers. But this is an outcome of unions' actions, not the determining factor.

In comparison, wage bargaining theories emphasise the trade union's role, but largely ignore the employer's. Almost all, explicitly or otherwise, make the assumption that his principal motivation in the wage bargaining process is to attempt to negotiate as low a wage as possible, thus ignoring the point, emphasised by excess demand theories, that employers will bear in mind the effect of the negotiated wage on the ease with which they can attract and retain labour over the contract period. Combining these two theories we arrive at the position that the employer will enter the wage negotiations with a wage he wishes to pay, which we will call the competitive wage. Similarly the trade union leader enters with a minimum wage he wishes to see negotiated, his target wage. If the competitive wage exceeds the union leader's target wage then this will be the negotiated wage. If, however, this is not the case then we are in a more genuine bargaining situation. The development of this synthesis will be undertaken in this chapter, beginning with the determinants of the employer's competitive wage. Into the theory will go elements from several strands of the literature — search, implicit contract, bargaining, even elements of permanent income theory will be absorbed. Out of it will emerge a theory capable of explaining why excess demand theories appeared to work so well prior to 1970, but not after that date. A summary of some of the notation we will use can be found in Table 2.1.

Table 2.1   *A guide to some of the notation used in this chapter*

Expression	Interpretation
λ_1	The number of interviews the job searcher expects to get in each period.
W_0^{e1t}	The maximum wage offer the job searcher can expect to receive after searching for t periods, expectations being held prior to search, that is, in period 0.
W_0^{e1N}	The maximum wage offer the job searcher expects to receive after searching for an optimal N periods, expectations being held prior to search. In effect this will be the worker's acceptance wage during the first period of search.
N	The optimal expected search duration for the job searcher.
λ_2	The number of interviews the employer expects to give in each period.
W_0^{e2t}	The minimum wage offer the employer can expect to be accepted after searching for a worker for t periods, expectations being held prior to search.
W_0^{e2n}	The minimum wage offer the employer can expect to be accepted after searching for an optimal n periods, expectations being held prior to search. In effect this will be the employer's acceptance wage during the first period of search. (Note, I was in some doubt as to whether to call this the employer's offer wage; I chose acceptance wage as this stresses the similarity with the job searcher's problem.)
n	The optimal duration of search for the employer.
π_0^{e2n}	The expected contribution to net revenue of a worker hired at a wage of W_0^{e2n}.
W_t^{e1N}	The acceptance wage of a worker who has already been searching for t periods. This is formed in exactly the same way as W_0^{e1N}, the difference being that this worker will have different perceptions of wages being offered due to the t unsuccessful periods of search.

Table 2.1 *continued*.............

Expression	Interpretation
γ	The minimum proportion of his membership the trade union leader will attempt to satisfy.
W_γ	The wage which, if negotiated, will just satisfy the aspirations of this proportion of his membership.

A Search Theoretic Model of Inflation and the Labour Market

In this section we shall develop a search theoretic approach to inflation along the lines of Phelps, Mortenson and Holt. As was made clear in the previous chapter, I feel that this approach offers the best chance of understanding the workings of the labour market, with particular reference to how it generates inflation. But in order to understand this, we must first answer the broader question of how the labour market allocates workers to jobs. There are three basic flow concepts through which this allocation takes place. These are hires and quits, which have been the subject of examination by Phelps and others, and fires, which have not been the subject of such keen examination. In our approach, the analysis of all three variables revolves narrowly around the concept of a wage aspiration level as a main determinant of individual decision making under imperfect knowledge.

This is essentially a subjective notion, reflecting the worker's perceptions of labour market conditions. In Holt's analysis it is determined by a constant mark-up on the worker's previous wage, falling with the length of time the worker remains unemployed. Thus to an extent this formulation ignores the central theme of search theory — that an individual can expect to find a better alternative state if he searches for a longer period. But information is not a free good, and while search is being undertaken income is not being earned; thus there is a trade-off. In determining his expected period of search the individual must balance these losses and gains so that he could not better his position by changing his expected duration of search. Thus, the individual's problem can be seen as having to determine his optimal expected period of search. However, as we shall see this also amounts to determining a wage offer which the unemployed worker is prepared to accept, for the two are jointly determined.

Of course, others have observed this problem, and as we saw in the previous chapter, a large body of literature on search theory has grown up.

A crucial assumption in this literature has been that search productivity is constant. I find this assumption altogether too limiting, and assume instead that the number of interviews an individual can expect to get in a given time period depends upon labour market conditions. We shall make several additional assumptions explicit here. First, that each interview results in an offer which the individual either accepts or rejects. Secondly, that although workers are not homogeneous in their talents, employers have no way of differentiating between them prior to hiring them. In addition, search is random and without recall. Individuals will be assumed to maximise net discounted income, firms net discounted profits, and both to be risk neutral. Furthermore, search is limited to the unemployed, and acceptance wages are revised at the end of each search period.

We begin with a result first established by Stigler (1962), that the more interviews received the higher the wage the individual can expect to be offered. Using Stigler's formulation we can specify the maximum wage offer the individual can expect to receive after searching for t periods as

$$W_0^{e1t} = \bar{W}_1 + \sigma_1 \sqrt{2 \log \lambda_1 t} \tag{2.1}$$

where λ_1 represents the expected number of interviews per period, $\bar{W}_1$ the mean of the distribution of the worker's expectations of wage offers, and σ_1 the variance of that distribution. Thus, the expected maximum wage offer increases with search, but at a decreasing rate. It will also vary with $\bar{W}_1$, σ_1 and λ_1. We can assume $\bar{W}_1$ to bear some relation to actual wages being offered to new workers by employers in the recent past and, as a simplifying assumption, σ_1 to be constant. It is, however, unlikely that λ_1 will be constant. It seems more reasonable to assume that the expected number of interviews per period will be positively related to the number of potential interviews, that is, vacancies, and perhaps inversely to the number of potential competitors for those interviews, that is, the unemployed. Thus the greater the number of vacancies the greater will be the number of expected interviews, which will increase the expected maximum wage offer at the end of each period of search, an increase in the number of unemployed having the opposite effect.

Having discussed what factors influence the wage aspiration level in a particular period, we will now attempt to analyse its role in the three labour market variables, quits, fires and hires, which we have specified. We shall begin with quits.

Quits
Given the assumptions we have made, an employed individual will quit his job if he expects to be better off in the long run by doing so, that is, if he

expects the discounted gain in income from accepting an alternative state to more than compensate him for the transition costs. We assume no direct search costs; therefore these will consist only of income forgone during search. Using discrete time we can illustrate this with the following inequality:

$$\sum_{i=1}^{N} (W_0 - B_i) \frac{1}{(1 + r_1)^i} < \sum_{i=N+1}^{I} (W_0^{e1N} - W_0) \frac{1}{(1 + r_1)^i} \quad (2.2)$$

The left-hand side measures total discounted income forgone during the expected period of search. This consists of the difference between his net current wage and any benefits he might qualify for while unemployed, summed and discounted over each period of search. The right-hand side measures total discounted gains. These are equivalent to the difference between the maximum wage he expects to be offered after an optimal period of search and his current wage discounted over the number of periods he expects to keep his new job. We assume that he starts work in the period immediately after finding that job; hence this equals $I-(N + 1)$, where I is the period in the future when he expects to leave that job.

The individual will quit if the inequality holds. This decision therefore depends upon present and expected wages, W_0 and W_0^{e1N}, the rate of discount r_1, any unemployment benefit he might qualify for, and I the date at which he expects to leave his new job. Of crucial importance is N, the expected number of periods he will have to devote to the search. This will be decided in the following manner. Take, for example, the situation where the individual is considering whether to spend two or three periods in expected search. The expected additional loss resulting from extending the expected search time by one period will be the best wage offer he could expect to get after searching for two periods less any benefits for which he might qualify. The expected additional gain will be the difference between the wage he expects to get after searching for three periods and that after searching for two, suitably discounted over the length of time he expects to hold the job. The individual will undertake this extra period of search if these gains outweigh the costs. In general, the optimal length of search, N, will be that number of periods where if the individual were to search for one more period, then for the first time expected losses would outweigh expected gains.

Hence we can determine the optimal length of time for being unemployed and searching once we know the expected maximum wage offer. On the other hand, we also know from equation (2.1) that t is a major determinant of the expected maximum wage offer. Both variables are thus interdependent, and combining equation (2.1) with the marginal equivalence conditions described in the previous paragraph gives a system in which N and W_0^{e1N} are simultaneously determined.

To acquire a better understanding of the system it may be useful to examine the effects of a change in vacancies, unemployment or benefits separately. An increase in vacancies or a decrease in unemployment will lead to an increase in the productivity of search, with the same amount of search time yielding a higher expected maximum wage offer. Thus inequality (2.2) is more likely to be satisfied and we can expect an increase in the number of quits. The effect of an increase in unemployment benefit has, as we saw in the literature, attracted considerable attention. Within the model being developed here it will have an immediate effect of reducing the cost of search. This will both lead to an increase in N, the optimal duration of expected search, an increase in W_0^{e1N} due to the increase in N, and once more an increase in the equilibrium number of quits.

These results are not much different from those reached by other theorists. In addition, what empirical work has been done tends, in general, to support them. However there is a likelihood that the effects of unemployment and vacancies on quits will be distorted at different phases of the cycle. Take, for example, the case when the economy moves out of a recession. There will be a 'backlog' of quits to be cleared before the equilibrium rate has been achieved, which will temporarily exaggerate the number of quits. This will occur both when there is a secular increase in wages and when individuals seek promotion as they gain experience. I shall illustrate it for the latter case and begin by making the assumption that the employed worker's perceptions of current wage offers are normally distributed, as in figure 2.1. W_0^{e1N} is defined as before, with N again being the expected period of search. The individual will not quit immediately his wage falls below W_0^{e1N}, due to search costs in the form of forgone income. Instead he will quit when his present wage falls below α, where this is determined by inequality (2.2).

As an individual gains experience in a job so he will begin to compare himself with those on the next rung of the ladder. Thus, after five years as an assistant office manager, he will begin to compare himself with managers of small offices, who in turn will compare themselves with managers of large offices, and so on and so forth. Therefore the mean wage of the group the individual compares himself with is continually drifting towards the right, dragging α with it. Consider now what happens as the economy moves out of recession, and, for example, the number of vacancies increases. This will increase the productivity of search, and the inequality defined in (2.2) is more likely to be satisfied. Therefore α will shift to the right to α'. Thus, all those individuals whose wages lie between these two points will now quit, this being in addition to the increase in the long-run level of quits generated by the increase in search productivity. These additional quits represent the backlog we have been discussing.

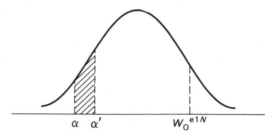

Figure 2.1   *The employed worker's perceptions of current wage offers*

Therefore, the initial effect of an increase in vacancies will be to increase quits above the new equilibrium level by an amount proportional to the shaded region in Figure 2.1. Once this increase has been absorbed quits will have risen to a new equilibrium rate at a higher level than the previous one. But this increase in the equilibrium level of quits will be greatly exaggerated in the initial stages of a boom. Similarly, as the economy moves into a recession there will be an exaggerated decline in quits.

Summarising, according to the theory so far developed, quits will depend upon the levels of vacancies and unemployment, cyclical changes in those variables, the rate at which future earnings are discounted, any benefit for which individuals might qualify, and the expectations of wages being offered for jobs for which they feel qualified. We will now turn to an examination of fires.

Fires
When a worker quits his job he does so in order to find a better one. The analysis of fires is slightly more complicated because there are several reasons for firing workers, perhaps the most common one being lack of demand for the goods they produce. This can arise for several reasons:

1 Due to a change in aggregate demand, that is, cyclical factors.
2 Due to seasonal factors.
3 Due to a changing pattern of aggregate demand, which leaves some industries expanding and others contracting.

4 Due to a changing pattern of production which leaves some firms expanding and others contracting.
5 Due to a changing locational pattern of production, as firms move from one area to another.

It is a combination of these factors which form the category known as layoffs, both permanent and temporary, which have been discussed by several writers. However, there is another category of fires, which has perhaps not received quite as much attention, and might be thought of as the analytical counterpart to quits. An employer may fire a worker, not because of changing demand conditions, but due to a desire to replace the worker with a better one. This decision is closely related to that of an employee who quits his job to replace it with a better one. We shall call this category of fires replacement fires, its analysis being similar to quits.

An employer will fire a worker if he believes that the discounted gains of doing so will outweigh the losses. The gains will be the expected increase in net revenue discounted over the expected duration of employment. The losses equal the amount which the fired worker would have contributed to net revenue over the expected length of search, plus any termination costs, such as redundancy payments. In algebraic notation the jth worker will be fired if the following inequality holds:

$$\sum_{i=1}^{n} \pi_j \frac{1}{(1+r_2)^i} + R_j < \sum_{i=n+1}^{E} (\pi_0^{e2n} - \pi_j) \frac{1}{(1+r_2)^i} \qquad (2.3)$$

π_j represents the expected net revenue contribution of the jth worker. π_0^{e2n} represents the expected contribution to net revenue of a worker hired at a wage of W_0^{e2n}. R_j represents any termination payments for the jth worker and r_2 is the employer's discount rate. E then represents the period in the future when employment is expected to be terminated for both fired worker and his expected replacement. This latter is a simplifying assumption. Its relaxation would open up some interesting insights into possible employer behaviour, but at the cost of making the analysis considerably more complex.

It can be seen from this that the introduction of redundancy payments will have made the employer in the UK less willing to fire unsatisfactory workers. This is not likely to be important for newly hired workers, and therefore mismatches, but it could become very significant for workers who become less satisfactory because of age.

It is also important to note that the contribution to net revenue the employer can expect a worker to make if he searches for t periods will increase as t increases. This is because the wage he can expect to pay falls with search time as shown by the following expression, which is again valid if the distribution of wages that job searchers will accept is normal.

$$W_0^{e2t} = \bar{W}_2 - \sigma_2\sqrt{2\log\lambda_2 t} \qquad (2.4)$$

The minimum pay offer which he can expect to be accepted after searching for t periods is a function of the mean, $\bar{W}_2$, and variance, σ_2, of his expectations concerning the distribution of workers' acceptance wages, and the expected number of interviews, λ_2, per period.

As before, it seems reasonable to assume that the expected number of potential interviews per period will be related to the number of vacancies relative to the number of unemployed. An increase in the number of vacancies, other things being equal, will lead to a decrease in the expected number of interviews per period that the employer can expect to obtain for his vacancy, while an increase in the number unemployed will have the opposite effect.

Given the analysis so far, we are now faced with a problem similar to the one already tackled in the section on quits, namely, how is the expected optimal period of search, in this case n, decided. As before, an individual will determine this so that he could not make himself better off by changing it. In the employer's case this will be immediately prior to when the expected losses from extending the search by one period exceed, for the first time, the expected gains. For period t, the expected losses equal the net revenue forgone from not having hired a worker after an expected $t-1$ search period, who would have contributed to revenue in period t. The expected gains equal the difference between the expected wages he would have to pay after having searched for $t-1$ and t periods, respectively, suitably discounted over the expected employment period.

Again we may wish to find the effects of a general increase in vacancies or a decrease in unemployment. Both will lead to a reduction in the productivity of search time. An employer who might be unwilling to change his habitual period of search can expect to have to pay higher wages in order to become a successful recruiter. He may, on the other hand, have to extend the expected period of search. A rational employer will probably do both. In any case it is clear that the costs of search are bound to rise in relation to the benefits. Inequality (2.3) is then less likely to be satisfied, and we can expect a reduction in the number of replacement fires. However, we should again note the probable existence of a backlog effect, for similar reasons as with quits.

A rather different reason for firing workers is to be found in a downward adjustment of the desired labour force, because of cyclical factors.

The extent to which an employer may reduce his labour force depends upon his expectations regarding the fall in demand, for both now and in the future, and on hiring conditions. Some employers may find it more profitable to hoard labour (Taylor, 1972). But for those employers who do decide to adjust their labour force, this adjustment can be brought about in two ways. They can fail to make good losses through voluntary quits, retirements, etc., or they can fire existing staff.

Another major category of firings will be those due to seasonal factors. In this case there is little scope for a trade-off relation between firing workers and not making good losses through natural wastage. There might be a relationship between the level of unemployment and seasonal firings as, given a constant workforce, if the economy is running at a high level then there will presumably be fewer seasonally unemployed people. But on the whole we might regard seasonal firings as being fairly constant.

The final category of firings will be those associated with a dynamic economy. There are several subcategories in this group; for example, workers might be fired due to a changing pattern of aggregate demand, due to changing technology, which does not affect all industries equally, or due to a changing geographical distribution of production.

Hires

Of the three concepts, hires, fires and quits, this is the most difficult to analyse as it depends upon the interaction of two sets of decision makers, employers and job searchers. We shall begin the analysis by presenting Holt's (1970) concept of acceptance curves, but in discrete time. The worker's acceptance curve is shown in Figure 2.2, and it plots his acceptance wage over the length of time he has been unemployed. In the first period of search the acceptance wage will be W_0^{e1N}. It equals the maximum wage offer he expects to receive after searching for N periods, where N is the optimal search time. We assume that the acceptance wage will not be constant, but will decline over the entire time the individual is unemployed, the justification being the Bayesian type adjustment process first put forward by Telser (1973). This reflects the fact that if the individual is still unemployed after the first period of search, then all the wage offers will have been less than his acceptance wage. Whereas if his prior distribution of wage offers had been correct there would have been the possibility of a wage offer in excess of his acceptance wage, which he would have accepted. He will therefore revise his perceptions of this distribution, probably adjusting the mean downwards. This reflects the fact that search performs two functions, the prime one being to find an acceptable offer of employment. But there is a secondary one of providing the individual with up-to-date information about the market. Thus in equation (2.1), $\bar{W}_1$ will be lower after the first period of search than it was before. This will then cause the acceptance wage in this second period of search to fall. The same process will be repeated at the end of the second period of search, and the third and fourth and so on, until the individual finds employment.

We also make the assumption that all job searchers, whether they quit their previous job or were fired, have the same acceptance curves. In our analysis there is no reason to suppose otherwise. The acceptance curve is derived from an income maximising process the parameters of which are presumably the same for both sets of searchers.

We can also derive an acceptance curve for the employer. This plots his acceptance wage against the length of time his vacancy remains unfilled. This is also shown in Figure 2.2. It can be seen that the employer's curve slopes upwards, the rationale for this being based upon the same Bayesian type adjustment process we have just used to justify the downward slope of the job searcher's acceptance curve. We assume that hiring can take place over R sub-periods of each full search period. We can then write the expected number of hires, H_0, that will take place from those vacancies which have been available for less than one full period, V_0, as:

$$H_0 = \sum_{r=0}^{R} V_{0r} P_{0r} \qquad (2.5)$$

V_{0r} represents the number of such vacancies open in the rth sub-period and P_r the probability of a single vacancy being filled. This probability will depend upon two factors: first, the probability of an interview in each sub-period and, secondly, the probability of such an interview resulting in an acceptable offer. In general, we would expect that the greater the average number of interviews in a full period of search, the greater will be the probability of an interview in any single sub-period. This, in turn, will be a function of the number of potential applicants in the form of the unemployed, and the number of vacancies which represent alternative openings for them. The probability of an interview proving successful, that is, the offer, which we assume always follows an interview, being accepted, will depend upon the acceptance wage of the job searcher, W_t^{e1N}, and that of the employer, W_0^{e2n}, where t in W_t^{e1N} varies from one job searcher to another, and is the number of periods for which each has been unemployed and searching. The relationship is straightforward, the probability of a successful interview equals the number of potential interviews that will result in successful offers, divided by the total number of potential interviews.

The interviews that will result in acceptable offers are those where the employee's acceptance wage is lower than that of an employer whose vacancy has been available for less than one full period of search. In Figure 2.2 this means job searchers who have been unemployed for four or more periods. The total number of potential interviews is simply equal to the total number of unemployed.

Figure 2.2   *The employer's and employee's acceptance curves*

An analysis can also be made to determine the number of hires made from those vacancies which have been unfilled for between one and two periods. These will have a higher probability of generating a successful offer, as the employer's acceptance wage with which they are associated will be greater than previously. Indeed it can be seen from Figure 2.2 that this wage will now prove acceptable to workers who have been searching for two or more periods. Further analysis can then be made about vacancies which have been open for even longer. The total number of hires in any one full period of search can then be found by summing hires over all such categories of vacancies:

$$H = \sum_{i=0}^{\infty} H_i = \sum_{i=0}^{\infty} \sum_{r=0}^{R} V_{ir} P_{ir} \qquad (2.6)$$

Thus, the total number of hires will be directly related to the total number of vacancies, as can be seen from equation (2.6). There will also be an indirect effect. An increase in the number of vacancies will, to a degree, reduce the probability of an interview taking place for any one vacancy, thus reducing the probability of a single vacancy being filled. However, it seems likely that the direct effect will prove dominant, and that as vacancies increase, so do the number of hires. The level of unemployment will also affect the number of hires, again through the effect on the probability of an interview taking place for a single vacancy, which it will increase. Thus, in this case, an increase in unemployment will, at least up to a limit, almost certainly cause an increase in hirings.

Besides depending upon the total numbers of unemployed and vacancies, hires will also vary with their age distribution. For instance, a sudden increase in vacancies will at first have a muted effect on hires as they will be characterised by an acceptance wage less than that of the average vacancy which has been unfilled for some time. The same remark applies to a sudden increase in the number unemployed, which will also cause hires to be below their equilibrium level.

Hires will also depend upon the position of the two acceptance curves in Figure 2.2. We have already seen that the employer's acceptance curve will depend upon average net revenue per worker, his discount rate, his expectations of both the number of interviews per period, which in turn will depend upon the levels of unemployment and vacancies, and the mean and variance of workers' acceptance wages. The employee's acceptance curve will depend upon any benefits for which he might qualify, his discount rate, his expectations of the probable number of interviews per period, and his expectations concerning the mean and variance of current wage offers.

The Implications for Inflation

What are the implications of all this for inflation? We can see that in a perfectly competitive labour market, wages would change for three reasons: first, due to workers being hired at different wages to those at which they were previously employed, or at which the job previously paid; secondly, workers being dissuaded from quitting by employers anxious to retain their services, and who offer them an increased wage to do so; finally, workers attempting to dissuade employers from firing them by offering their services at a reduced wage. We shall examine these in turn.

The hiring wage, that is, the average wage at which workers are hired, will depend on the position of the typical employer's acceptance curve in Figure 2.2. This will be determined by his expectations concerning job searchers' acceptance wages, the number of unemployed job searchers, and the number of vacancies competing for their attention, and the speed with which employers want to fill vacancies. An increase in expectations about workers' acceptance wages will shift the curve upwards. These will be related to expectations concerning other employers' acceptance wages, because job searchers will themselves take these into consideration, but the two will not be identical. An increase in the number of job searchers, or a reduction in the number of competing vacancies, will increase the efficiency of search for the employer, thus causing his initial acceptance wage to decline. But, it may also lead to a more steeply increasing acceptance curve, as more information per period is fed into the Bayesian type adjustment process by which the acceptance wage is revised from period to period. Increased search productivity should also lead to a reduction in the average time a vacancy remains unfilled, which will further cause a reduction in the hiring wage, as the employer's acceptance wage increases with the length of time the vacancy remains unfilled. Finally, as we saw when discussing fires, the employer's acceptance wage will be related to the revenue forgone in having an unfilled vacancy. The greater this is, the quicker he will want the vacancy filled and the higher will be the acceptance wage.

The hiring wage will also depend upon the position of the typical employee's acceptance curve in Figure 2.2. The lower this is relative to the typical employer's acceptance curve, the greater is the probability of an employer's offer proving acceptable. The position of this curve will be determined by the job searchers' expectations about wages employers will be offering, the speed with which they want to obtain work, the number of job opportunities, that is, vacancies, and the number of potential competitors for those opportunities, that is, the unemployed. An increase in expectations concerning employers' acceptance wages will shift the job searcher's acceptance curve upwards, thereby reducing the probability that an employer's offer will prove acceptable, and increasing the hiring wage. The speed with which job searchers will want to obtain work will be related to the costs of search, as we saw when discussing quits. The greater are these costs the shorter will be the optimal search period, and the lower will be the job searcher's acceptance wage. The cost of search in our model is forgone income while unemployed and searching. This will be related to the level of unemployment benefits or insurance relative to net earnings. An increase in this ratio will reduce the cost of search and push up the job searcher's acceptance curve, thus increasing the hiring wage. An increase in the number of job searchers, or a reduction in the number of vacancies will make search less productive for the job searcher, and hence tend to reduce both his initial acceptance wage and the rate at which the acceptance curve declines. There will be a further effect, as before, in that this will also tend to increase the average time spent searching for a job, which will tend to move the job searcher further down his acceptance curve, thus again reducing the hiring wage.

There are two other channels by which labour market conditions can affect the wage rate, one important one being through their effect on quits. Indeed this is the transmission mechanism favoured by Phelps (1968) himself. He put forward the hypothesis that firms in setting the contract wage would take into account conditions in the labour market, as these would determine the number of quits over the period in which the contract is operative. The firm then sets the contract wage taking into account the likely number of quits, and also presumably the likely costs of those quits in terms of lost production while not having the job filled, and balancing these costs against the costs of increasing the contract wage. This is an approach to which we shall return later. But first, we will turn to an analysis which has more in common with that of the hiring wage which we have just completed.

The underlying idea behind this analysis is that when an employee informs an employer that he wishes to quit, the employer may respond by making him an improved offer in the hope of making the job sufficiently attractive to retain his services. It is this wage, when accepted, that we call the quit wage. The employer would do this if, in discounted terms, the cost of this course of action was less than the cost of hiring a new worker. Turning to equation (2.2) we can see that the decision to quit depends partly upon the present wage, which is a significant factor in both the expected costs and gains of search. Therefore, if the present wage is increased, this will increase the cost of search and reduce the gains, and such action may well persuade the worker to remain in his present job.

So much is fairly obvious, but what is not so obvious is how much the employer will be prepared to offer to tempt the worker to remain in his service. Using the notation and terminology previously defined, the employer will be prepared to increase the wage as long as, in discounted terms, the benefit of doing so outweighs the cost. This can be expressed in algebraic form by slightly modifying inequality (2.3) to

$$\sum_{i=1}^{n} \pi_j' \frac{1}{(1+r_2)^i} > \sum_{i=n+1}^{E} (\pi_0^{e2n} - \pi_j') \frac{1}{(1+r_2)^i} \qquad (2.7)$$

where j denotes the jth worker who has just informed the employer of his intention to quit and π_j' is his net revenue contribution at a wage of W_j'. The left-hand side of the expression represents the discounted cost of forgone revenue during the expected period of search. The right-hand side represents the expected gains, which may be negative, of not employing the jth worker at the wage W_j', but of searching for a replacement. As long as the cost outweighs the gains, the employer will be willing to increase W_j'. The upper limit to what the employer is prepared to offer is reached when the inequality is no longer satisfied. It should perhaps also be noted that in practice there may well be training costs involved in hiring a new worker which will tend to increase the quit wage even further.

There are several implications arising out of this analysis, some obvious and some not so obvious. First, the longer the expected period of search, the greater will be the cost of forgone revenue, provided that π_j' is positive to begin with, and hence the higher the wage the employer will be prepared to offer. Similarly, the more productive the worker, the greater will be π_j', which will again tend to increase the wage the employer will be prepared to offer.

If we further assume that the jth worker has an average productivity, then when W_j' equals the employer's initial acceptance wage, that is, the wage he expects to have to pay to hire a replacement worker, the term $(\pi_0^{e2n} - \pi_j')$ on the right-hand side of (2.7) is automatically zero. Therefore, provided that at this wage π_j' is positive, the inequality will be satisfied. Indeed, it is probable that it will continue to be satisfied at certain wage levels above the acceptance wage. We thus get the interesting result that the limit to the wage an employer is prepared to offer in such circumstances will exceed the wage he initially expects to have to pay in the hiring market. This possible premium exists because the expected cost of replacing that worker is not just the wage he expects to have to pay in the hiring market, but also his forgone contribution during the expected period of search. The actual hiring wage will, unless the vacancy is filled immediately, exceed the employer's initial acceptance wage. None the less the existence of this premium points to the possibility that there may also be a premium of the quit wage over the hiring wage. The minimum wage that will prove acceptable to the worker can be inferred from (2.2). Even a fractional increase will prevent this inequality from being satisfied, and deter the worker from quitting in the immediate future. We therefore have an upper and lower limit to the quit wage. The exact point within this range which will be agreed upon may depend on bargaining factors. It might also depend on the employer's expectations concerning the rate of change of the hiring wage and other conditions in the hiring market. If he anticipates it increasing rapidly, then he may increase the employee's wage more substantially than he otherwise would to delay a reoccurence of the same problem, a frequent revision of employees' wages presumably incurring costs to the employer in their own right. For all these reasons the quit wage will depend upon events in the hiring market. It will therefore be a function of the same variables as the hiring wage, although not necessarily in the same way.

There is a third mechanism by which wages might change, which concerns the reaction of a worker under the threat of being fired. The jth worker, faced with dismissal because his productivity and wage rate are such that the inequality defined in (2.3) holds, could offer his labour at a lower wage rate so that the inequality no longer holds. A lower limit will again be set by that worker's initial acceptance wage, suitably adjusted for forgone income during the expected period of search. An upper limit to this wage will be set by the necessity that it invalidates (2.3).

It should be noted that there are two possible reasons why this inequality might hold in the first place. First, the jth worker may have a lower than average level of productivity, in which case it is possible that he has been dismissed several times in the past, with the possibility that he will be dismissed again when he is hired for a new job. With this in mind the worker may well accept a lower wage to that suggested above. Secondly, the worker's wage rate may be higher than average. Perhaps he was hired at a time when the employer had difficulty in filling a vacancy because the market was tight, or alternatively it might be that all wages are falling in a recession.

According to the analysis so far developed, the average wage rate will change because some workers change jobs and other, potentially mobile, workers have their wages revised. The principal determinants of wage changes to the mobile and potentially mobile will be the levels of unemployment and vacancies, average net revenue contribution per worker, unemployment benefits and expectations of wage changes in the hiring market. In addition to the size of increase given to the mobile and potentially mobile, changes in the wage index will also be a function of the number of such workers, that is, the number of workers hired and the number of deterred quits and fires, all of which will be functions of the same basic labour market variables already mentioned.

Integration of Search and Implicit Contract Theory

Thus far we have established a theory which generates wage increases to the mobile and potentially mobile, that is, to those who change jobs and eventually to the rest of the labour force. Before turning to examine the role of implicit contract theory in determining the employer's competitive wage, it is perhaps worth considering some aspects of the pure search theoretic model we have developed in more detail. First, we will consider what happens as the economy moves out of a recession. The initial increase in vacancies will make hiring more difficult for the employer by reducing the number of interviews per period he can expect to receive. This, in turn, will increase both the optimal length of search and his initial acceptance wage. Partly because of this the hiring wage will also rise. This increase in the hiring wage, together with an increase in the number of vacancies, will cause an increase in the number of quits, which will be particularly marked if the recession has been prolonged; in which case there will be a backlog of quits to clear up. Faced with these quits the employer will attempt to persuade the worker to remain in his employ by increasing his wage. If the boom continues then every worker, even the least productive, will have received a wage increase, either from his present employer or by changing jobs. A reverse process would operate when the economy moves into a recession, with generally falling wages in the hiring market being disseminated throughout the entire labour force via the firing mechanism.

It is also of some interest to reflect on the degree of keenness with which employers will want to fill vacancies. This will be directly related to the net revenue contribution per worker, and if profits in general are buoyant then this too will be high, causing employers to be anxious to retain and attract labour. Profits will vary in a cyclical fashion; there may also be longer-run trends. In the UK, for example, there has, in the postwar years, been superimposed upon cyclical fluctuations a long-run secular decline in profits. This would have tended to reduce the rate of inflation consistent with given values of other labour market variables. But there is likely to be a second secular effect connected with the growth in labour productivity. This will have the effect of increasing the net revenue contribution per worker, and hence lead to an upward drift in the wage equation. More specifically the growth in labour productivity makes each worker more productive, thus increasing the cost to an employer of having an unfilled vacancy. In an attempt to fill the vacancy more rapidly he will increase his acceptance wage. Similarly, when faced with a worker who wishes to quit, he will be prepared to offer him a higher wage to retain his services. This conclusion, which as far as I am aware has not been reached elsewhere, is I believe of some importance.

Also of interest is the coefficient on expectations. The importance of this has, of course, been stressed by many other theorists. But nearly all assume a unit coefficient in order that an employer may maintain his desired differential over what he expects other employers to be paying. However, on reflection it becomes apparent that this will only succeed in maintaining the absolute differential. An example may clarify this. If an employer wishes to maintain a differential over other employers of 10 per cent, and they are paying £20, then he will have to pay £22. If, however, he expects them to increase their wages by 5 per cent to £21, then in order to maintain a desired differential of 10 per cent he will have to pay £23.1. If he were merely to increase his wages by the desired differential plus any expected percentage increase in wages, he would pay £23, which would merely succeed in maintaining an absolute differential of £2, but not a relative one of 10 per cent. It is my belief that the ease with which labour can be retained and attracted is related to the relative and not the absolute differential. In addition I believe that this interpretation is more in keeping with the spirit of search models. Thus the coefficient on expectations is not constant but a variable equal to unity plus the desired differential, in the above example being equal to 1.1. Within the context of the model we have developed this conclusion arises from the assumption that the variance of the distribution of workers' acceptance wages increases in proportion to the mean. For the constant unit coefficient on expectations to be valid, this variance would also need to be constant.

The theory has been neoclassical in nature with many strong assumptions being made; for example, that job searchers are restricted to the unemployed and that employers cannot differentiate between workers prior to hiring them. None the less several interesting and in my view plausible conclusions have emerged from the analysis, which cannot be found elsewhere. The role of profits within an excess demand framework has not previously been stressed, neither has the concept of a backlog of quits as the economy moves out of a recession, nor the possibility of a non-unit, variable coefficient on expectations been discussed elsewhere. In addition, the analysis of hires has illuminated the interactive nature of the search process.

We now turn to considerations which arise from the implicit contract literature. These have so far been ignored, as I wanted to highlight the search theoretic approach, and the differences between it and standard search theories. However, it is clear that the employer, when determining wage rates, will have in mind other factors besides the immediate effects on his ability to hire and retain labour. He will in effect wish to pay workers a wage which they consider fair. He will do this for several reasons. First, by paying such a wage he will gain a reputation as a fair employer, which will enable him to achieve a given labour force at a lower wage rate than would otherwise be the case, this argument being similar to those of Hicks (1963) and Feldstein (1976) already discussed. However, there is a further effect which has not received so much attention in the literature. If the employer pays workers less than a fair wage then this may well cause resentment amongst them which will be reflected in their work standards.

For example, the number of rejects in a manufacturing process may rise, or in a service industry standards of service may fall. This is something that the employer will be aware of and take into consideration when setting wage rates.

To examine exactly how such considerations combine with our search theory, let us consider the example of when the economy is moving into a recession. We shall assume for the moment that wages in the hiring market are falling below the wages of the employer's current workforce. So that on pure search theoretic grounds it may be optimal for the employer to threaten some of that workforce with dismissal unless they take a cut in their wages. The gains of such a course of action will be the reduction in the wage bill. The costs will be threefold. First, he will damage his reputation as a fair employer. He will therefore, in the future, have to pay higher wage rates in order to maintain his labour force at a given level. Secondly, he will cause resentment amongst his workforce which will reduce their effective productivity. Thirdly, he will reduce the ease with which he can retain and attract labour. Even though this is being reduced to its search theoretic optimum, this is still a cost which must be balanced against the gains. The effect of all this will be to add two further elements to the left-hand side of (2.3), reflecting the costs and degree of both the increased resentment amongst his workforce and the loss of reputation as a fair employer. The result is that a wage–productivity combination, which previously would have just satisfied the inequality, will no longer do so. The employer will no longer be as willing to fire or threaten to fire workers in a recession so as to reduce his wage bill, although in the case of a newly hired worker who proves to be below average productivity, there may be no such change in the inequality. In this case neither the employer's reputation nor the morale of his workforce may be harmed at the threatened dismissal of such a worker.

Of course employers faced with the same set of data should reach the same conclusion, and in this case all achieve the same degree of fairness. Differences could be introduced by assuming that not all employers will be faced with the same set of product market conditions. In this case the costs of firing workers in terms of forgone profits during search will vary from firm to firm. For a firm with wide product market variations, these costs will also vary widely, and hence the likelihood of a given worker facing dismissal at some time within the cycle will be greater than for a firm within a more stable environment. The job searcher will then have to evaluate the employer's reputation for 'fairness' as well as his wage offer. If the reputation of the employer is good, then the gains from search as evaluated by the job searcher will stand a greater chance of extending indefinitely into the future. If his reputation is not so good, then the job searcher can expect the gains to be more short-lived. He may also anticipate only a short period of employment with that firm. Under the income-maximising assumptions we have made these two cases must yield equal, expected, discounted income streams to the job searcher.

Alternatively it is possible that the worker cannot distinguish between fair and 'unfair' employers, in which case the analysis concerning hires is relatively unchanged. But the quit decision is not. The right-hand side of (2.2) will now consist of two sets of income streams, one for fair employers and the other for unfair employers. These will be multiplied by the probabilities associated with finding a fair or unfair employer. This, for any given hiring wage, will reduce the expected gains from search. Thus for a fair employer the worker will be less likely to quit. However, for an unfair employer the reverse will be the case, as individuals will be anticipating that in future recessions they will once more be faced with the choice of dismissal or a wage reduction. They will then take this into account when evaluating their present position compared with alternatives in the hiring market.

There is a certain asymmetry in the above analysis. There are advantages to an employer in appearing to be fair, in not taking advantage of a slack labour market to reduce his wage bill. But there are no such advantages for the employee to be 'fair'. This would be changed if, for example, employers could make some evaluation of a job searcher prior to hiring him. In this case that worker's 'loyalty record' would be an important consideration. This asymmetry is also at odds with much of implicit contract theory which assumes the existence of a contract which both parties abide by. In our analysis there is no such contract; both parties act in their own interest unbound by past events. One effect of this asymmetry is that the clearest impact of contract theory will be on replacement fires. These and the wage changes associated with them will be less likely to occur.

However, there is now an additional reason for wages to change, which we shall now examine. We begin by assuming that the fair wage we have spoken of is one that will equate the workers' standard of living to some target level. Now suppose something occurs, for example, a price increase, such that this standard of living is now less than the target level. The employer will then have an incentive to increase the wages of his workforce towards the target level. The advantages of doing so are once again linked with the morale of his workforce and his reputation as a fair employer. The costs are the increased wages he has to pay. It should be noted that this will probably not necessitate his increasing wages up to the workers' target level. Instead he will, as always, balance the costs and gains involved and equate them at the margin. This is a most important concept, and one which lies at the heart of this analysis on inflation.

Thus we can see that when the fair wage is greater than the wage the employer would wish to pay on pure search grounds implicit contract considerations become highly relevant in determining the wage the employer wishes to pay. They are also likely to be of some importance when the reverse is the case. Then, when the employer considers increasing his wage rates to retain and attract labour he must also take into consideration the possible future effects on the fair wage. If, as we shall be arguing later, this is formed by reference to past wage rates, then increasing wages at time t will increase the fair wage in future periods. His reaction to this will partly depend upon his expectations regarding future labour market conditions. He will probably be less concerned if he expects the tight labour market conditions to continue than if he does not. But even in the latter case he will still probably increase wage rates. The benefits of doing so are in the present, whilst the costs are in the future and will to some extent be discounted. This is especially so if, as seems likely, fair wages are a lagged function of real wage rates. In this case an increase in the real wage now will have its full effects on fair wages only over a number of periods.

Thus we can see that implicit contract considerations tend to reduce the fluctuations in wages which would arise from pure search considerations. In addition there is reason to believe that these effects will be greatest when the fair wage exceeds the wage that would be paid on search grounds alone. For in this case the costs of 'breaking the contract' are both immediate and indefinite, whereas the gains only relate to the present period. When the reverse is true the implicit contract costs of increasing wages on search grounds are in the future, and hence to an extent discounted, whereas the benefits lie in the present. Thus a useful approximation we can think of search factors being dominant when the fair wage is less than the wage that would be paid on search grounds, and implicit contract factors being dominant otherwise.

Fair Wages

The above analysis assigned a critical role to a fair wage, and it is this which we shall now examine. It was suggested earlier that a fair wage would be one that would equate a worker's standard of living with some target level. This is in accord with a suggestion made by Okun (1975) and also with some elements in the bargaining literature, for example,

Ashenfelter and Johnson (1969) and Johnston and Timbrell (1973), although within a slightly different context. Often the idea is that the worker will aspire to a wage that will enable him to maintain a constant standard of living, although much of the recent literature argues that workers will be aiming for an increased standard of living.

It will be suggested that the money wage workers aspire to is one that will enable them to maintain their standard of living. It will also be suggested that this is quite compatible with them attempting to secure an increased real wage. We begin the analysis by examining Friedman's (1957) theory of the consumption function. He suggested that people base their consumption upon a concept he called permanent income. If this is correct, and if it is also correct that individuals attempt to maintain their standard of living, then it follows that the income concept individuals will be concerned with is their permanent income, and it is this which they will attempt to maintain. Friedman, in constructing a variable to measure permanent income, suggested the following formula

$$Y_{\mathrm{p}}(T) = \beta \int_{-\infty}^{T} e^{(\beta - \alpha)(t - T)} Y(t) dt \qquad (2.8)$$

where β is the adjustment coefficient by which permanent income adjusts to measured income, and α is the estimated rate of growth of real income. Friedman added this as he thought it more reasonable to estimate permanent income in two parts: first, a trend value which is taken to grow at a constant percentage rate, and secondly, a weighted average of adjusted deviations of past values.

However, it would seem that this formulation does not really capture the spirit of the permanent income hypothesis, which is that in making consumption plans individuals do not just consider the present. Rather they will form a plan defining expected consumption levels for a considerable time in the future, the plan being constrained by income levels expected over a similar time period. It is true that there is a growth factor present in Friedman's formulation, but it is purely retrospective. It does not extend into the future, merely adjusting previous periods' income to put them on a comparable basis with present income. It in no manner allows for expected income growth in the future. Thus in making their permanent income calculations individuals perceive that income has been growing in the past, allow for this when calculating permanent income, but apparently believe that all such growth ends in the present period.

If we turn to the text to see whether this is consistent with Friedman's view, or to see if he made an error in presenting the formula, then we run into difficulties. For apart from the mathematical definition of permanent income we have just given, an exact economic interpretation is surprisingly difficult to find. He does not seem to favour the view (see Friedman, 1957, p. 25) that permanent income is equal to the present value of the individual's present and future earnings plus his non-human capital. This he rejects on the grounds that it implies an extremely long time horizon. He also doubts whether individuals can borrow on the basis of anticipated returns from both human and non-human wealth at the same rate of interest at which they can lend accumulated non-human wealth. On the other hand, he also rejects the possibility that individuals take no account of future income, on the grounds that this is too short-sighted. Instead he seems to favour an intermediate view.

Alternative theories of the consumption function have favoured the first view, although the possibility of future secular income growth is similarly discounted in the corresponding empirical work. Thus Ando and Modigliani's (1963) life-cycle hypothesis seems very similar to the hypothesis that people base their expenditure plans on the discounted present value of their present and future earnings. However this may be, it is clear that unless one takes the extreme view, which Friedman himself rejects, that no account at all is taken of the future, then (2.8) is not a valid proxy for permanent income. For although it allows for a retrospective growth factor it fails to extend this into the future. The growth element in (2.8) merely adjusts previous periods' income to comparable terms with present income. His measurement then is merely a filter for extracting temporary deviations from permanent components, which it achieves by taking a weighted average of lagged income suitably adjusted for secular income growth.

Yet none the less we may build upon Friedman's initial insight that individuals, in making their consumption plans, take account of income over an extended time horizon, and that these expenditure plans relate to a similar time horizon. In this case it becomes clear that a real wage increase can only succeed in maintaining a worker's standard of living if it is consistent with previously held expectations concerning income growth. A wage increase less than this will involve a reduction in a worker's standard of living in the sense that his consumption plans will need to be revised downwards. Expectations of future income will in general (we shall be discussing exceptions later) be based upon present and past income trends. One possibility is that previous real wage rates are merely extrapolated into the future. Alternatively more sophisticated Box–Jenkins type mechanisms may be employed. Both of these methods are different to the one Friedman employed, which as we have seen was essentially a weighted average of present and past income levels. The methods I have suggested are more flexible in as much as they will both, implicitly, take account of different growth rates in measuring present income's permanent component, as well as extrapolating it into the future.

A fair wage will then be one that leaves consumption plans unchanged. In the simplest case, where past trends are extrapolated into the future, it will equal the extrapolated wage from one period ago. The desired real wage increase will then be the difference between the fair wage and the present actual wage. The gross desired money wage increase will also need to take account of expected inflation over the period for which the wage will be effective. Account may also have to be taken of the fact that within a progressive tax system any desired increase in wages net of tax will necessitate a greater increase in gross wages. Alternatively the employer may take the view that it is not encumbent upon him to correct variations in income due directly to government action.

Employer's Competitive Wage

The employer's competitive wage is the wage the employer will want to negotiate with the union. As its name implies it will be related to the wages the employer would wish to pay in a competitive labour market in the absence of a trade union, the analysis of which we have just considered. However, we may expect the analysis that emerges from including trade unions to differ from that made previously for several reasons. First, we would expect a move towards regular collective bargaining, and out of this would arise the concept of a wage rate in some way applicable to all workers, and set for some, probably fixed, time into the future. This differs from the previous analysis in several respects. First, there was previously no limit on the frequency with which wages could be changed. Thus, faced with changed labour market conditions, the employer could take immediate action in the form of changing his hiring wages and increasing the wages of workers who threaten to quit. To some extent this flexibility has gone, although it may still be possible for him to pay wage rates above the negotiated rate to certain workers. However, it is unlikely that he will be able to do the reverse, namely, pay lower rates to less productive workers. Hence we get the result that in a unionised firm, an employee faced with dismissal no longer has the opportunity of offering his services at a lower wage rate.

In the case where no deviation from the negotiated wage is possible the employer in deciding upon his competitive wage will take into account the effect of the negotiated wage upon the ease with which he can attract and retain labour during the contract period. We assume, as always, that he will determine the competitive wage by setting it at such a level that the marginal benefit of changing it will equal the marginal cost. The marginal cost will be the increase in the wage bill. The marginal benefits relate to the decrease in net revenue forgone as a result of the increased ease of hiring and retaining labour. The reduction in quits the employer could expect will cause a reduction in lost revenue while searching for replacement workers. In addition the reduction in search time while looking for replacement workers, or filling new jobs caused by an expansion in the desired labour force, will also cause a reduction in net revenue forgone as a result of unfilled vacancies.

This will then be the employer's competitive wage, that is, the wage he wishes to negotiate with the union, provided that it equals or exceeds the fair wage. If it does not then the search theoretic arguments described above will lose some of their relevance. The employer in negotiating with the union will then wish to agree upon a wage somewhere between the two. He will take into account the costs of paying a wage less than the fair wage and balance these against the gains. The gains will relate once more to the reduced wage bill. The costs will be connected with the damage to his reputation as a fair employer, the reduction in the morale of his workforce and the increased difficulty he will have in retaining and hiring labour. Other things being equal we would expect that the greater the gap between the optimal search theoretic wage and the fair wage, the more his competitive wage will fall short of the fair wage.

In the case where the employer is allowed to pay wages above the negotiated rates to certain individual workers there will be no gains to an employer, in search theoretic terms, from an increase in the negotiated wage rate. In this case it would appear that the impact of the union is much less than in the previous case, at least as regards the employer's competitive wage. However, we shall largely ignore this in the remainder of the analysis. We now turn to examine the bargaining problem from the trade union side.

The Trade Union Leader's Target Wage

We shall approach this stage of the analysis in a similar vein to Ross (1948) and Ashenfelter and Johnson (1969). In particular it will be argued that the prime concern of union leaders is to maintain their job. This is not necessarily a cynical attitude; they may well also be motivated by higher ideals, but in order to have any chance of achieving these they must first maintain their position. This will necessitate satisfying some minimum proportion, γ, probably in excess of a half, of the union membership with which he is directly concerned. With respect to wage negotiations this will imply satisfying at least that proportion of his membership's wage aspirations. It is assumed that these aspirations are formed in a manner similar to that already discussed when analysing the fair wage. More specifically it is the wage just sufficient to keep the worker's consumption plan, based on permanent income considerations, unchanged. The union leader's target wage, W_γ, will then be the one that just satisfies the aspirations of this minimum proportion of his membership.

These aspiration wages will not be the same for all workers. They will differ due to differences in the way individuals derive their permanent income, for example, due to different adjustment coefficients. There will also be differences in expected inflation rates. Hence trade union leaders will be faced with a membership that has a distribution of wage aspirations as shown in Figure 2.3. From this it can be seen that the greater is γ the greater will be the union leader's target wage. In addition provided γ is in excess of 50 per cent, the target wage will also increase with the variance of the distribution in Figure 2.3. However, at the same time opposition to this target wage will increase from those with aspiration wages in excess of the target wage.

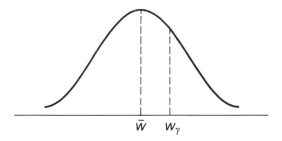

Figure 2.3   *Distribution of union members' aspiration wages*

The variance itself will be a function of the variances which make up the component elements of the desired money wage, that is, the desired real wage and expectations of inflation. Both of these are likely to increase in periods of perceived change, for example, when real income growth slows down at the beginning of a recession, or when inflation suddenly starts accelerating after a period of relative stability. Differences in the degree of certainty with which individuals hold their expectations of inflation will have no effect on the individual's aspiration wage as we have built the theory around income maximising individuals. If, however, we were to replace this with utility maximising individuals, where the utility function defined on the real wage is strictly concave, that is, it exhibits diminishing marginal utility with respect to the real wage, then the standard von Neumann–Morgenstern (1947) expected utility framework could be employed, with the result that the existence of individual uncertainty with respect to the real wage would reduce the expected utility of that wage. Therefore in order to maintain a given level of utility the individual must increase his aspiration wage. Individual uncertainty in this context will again be related to the rate of inflation, and uncertainty over this will lead to uncertainty about the real wage over the contract period. This kind of uncertainty is also likely to increase when there is a period of perceived structural change, of the kind defined in the next chapter, in the inflation rate.

If we now place this discussion within the context of the early 1970s, in either the UK or the USA, and recall that at this time inflation had accelerated sharply, then we would expect to see individual workers aspiring to real wage increases that would overcompensate for any expected price increase. We would also expect to witness trade union leaders attempting to negotiate settlements that would increasingly exceed the average aspiration wage of their membership. Yet at the same time we would expect to see increased opposition to such settlements by those of the membership whose aspiration wage lies to the right of W_γ. This might lead trade union leaders into attempting to reduce this opposition by securing settlements that would satisfy a greater proportion of their membership. It might also provide a platform upon which aspirants to the leadership, both official and unofficial, could build their case, or breakaway movements be formed. Such events could easily be interpreted as increasing trade union militancy amongst both the rank and file and the leadership, and that this would be a direct cause of inflation. Whereas, in fact, such militancy would be a symptom, not a cause, of inflation.

An Analysis of the Wage Bargaining Process

We now have all the elements of the problem and can illustrate how they interact in the actual wage bargaining process. We have suggested that the employer will have in mind an optimal wage that he wishes to negotiate, based on the difficulties of attracting and retaining labour and his reputation as a fair employer. This wage we have called the competitive wage. If this is in excess of the trade union leader's target wage then there is no problem; this will then be the negotiated wage, that is, the actual wage negotiated between employer and union. If, however, this is not the case, then the situation is more complex. The employer will probably be willing to increase his wage offer above the competitive wage rather than incur a strike. Exactly how much further he will be willing to go will depend upon the relative gains and losses of incurring a strike. The principal gain, perhaps the only one, is the reduction in the negotiated wage brought about by the strike. In the first instance this reduction will be valid only over the period for which the contract is negotiated. However, it is conceivable that in certain circumstances the employer might envisage a strike now as affecting the negotiating position of unions in future negotiations. Hence the envisaged gains may extend for some time into the future.

The closer is the wage that could be negotiated in the absence of a strike to the employer's competitive wage, then the smaller will be these gains. This will be so for two reasons: first, the smaller will be the reduction in the negotiated wage which the employer will be seeking to secure, and secondly, there are advantages to the employer in exceeding his competitive wage, in the sense that he will find it increasingly easy to retain and attract labour. Within the region of the competitive wage these gains will be close to the costs in terms of a higher wage bill. Thus for wages slightly above the competitive wage the net gain from a reduction in the negotiated wage will be relatively small in comparison with the direct costs of the strike.

This potential gain will be more important the greater is the share of labour in total costs. Thus in a highly capital intensive industry, where labour costs are a relatively small component of total costs, the gains from incurring a strike will tend to be less than in a labour intensive industry. In the case where the strikers are only a small proportion of the total workforce, but the wage award they get will influence the negotiating position of the rest of the workforce, then the gains to the employer will be increased. A similar case occurs when the employer has several different firms or plants, and the average award in any one will set the pattern for the remainder. An example of when the costs to the employer may be disproportionate to the number of strikers is where they have the potential to halt all production, for example, the case of a small group of skilled men.

The expected losses to the employer of incurring a strike will be the immediate expected difference in profits due to the strike. These will be reduced for several reasons. First there will be the loss in profits due to the cessation of supplies. These will of course be greater the larger are profits in general and will also vary directly with the expected duration of the strike. But there will also be other factors to consider. If stocks are low these losses will be more severe than if stocks are high. We might expect stocks to be highest at sometime in the downswing of the cycle when employers have produced more goods than they can sell. In such cases the reduction in profits from lost sales may be negligible. Indeed it may even be that this presents the employer with a convenient way to cut back production and reduce those stocks. Hence both the general profit level and the level of stocks will be important in determining short-run costs to the employer of lost sales. In the longer run there may be losses even when the strike has ended. These may occur if buyers, either consumers or other firms, are able to find alternative suppliers of the product. The more easily this can be done, that is, the greater is the substitutability of one supplier for another, then the greater the risk of sales being lost and profits being affected even once the strike has ended. Similarly, even if the employer has a monopoly of this particular product, if close substitutes are available then again there might be a more permanent reduction in sales.

On a slightly different plane there will be the potential reduction in workers' productivity following a strike. This might serve to introduce a bad industrial relations atmosphere into the firm which may have a semi-permanent effect on profits. In addition there is a possibility that strikers will find alternative full-time employment, in which case when the strike ends the employer will have a reduced labour force, and may have to hire more workers to replace them — a process that will incur him further costs. He will also risk losing his reputation as a fair employer. Indeed as he would be in open conflict with his workforce over wages this would almost certainly be so. Once lost, such a reputation would take a long time to rebuild, and as a consequence he can expect in the long run to have to pay higher wage rates than would otherwise be the case. An interesting consequence of this is that having once incurred a strike, and lost his reputation for fairness, this will no longer weigh in the balance in future negotiations. He will then be more willing to incur a strike than other employers who have a good reputation.

The time horizon for these costs varies from the length of the strike for lost output to an indefinite period for some of the other costs. Of equal interest is the relevant time horizon for the benefits. Ashenfelter and Johnson use an indefinitely long one, implying of course that the benefits last indefinitely. More realistically we might recognise that any particular negotiated wage will only last over the contract period, after which a new one will be agreed, and therefore it would seem possible that the expected benefits would only last over the contract period. On the other hand, an employer may well feel that a strike will not only reduce the trade union leader's target wage in this negotiation, but in future ones as well. This will occur if, for example, the occurrence of a strike has a downward impact effect on the permanent income calculations in future years. In addition the actual reduction in real wages secured by a strike in this period will have a direct effect on future permanent income calculations independent of any impact effect. Thus the employer can quite legitimately expect the benefits to be spread over several contracts.

The employer will once more be faced with a dual decision process. He must first calculate the expected duration of the strike, which will in part depend upon the wage he is willing to offer to end it. He can then use this to calculate the reduction in the negotiated wage which he can expect the strike to bring about. Besides the factors already discussed, these will also depend on the speed with which the employer expects the negotiated wage to fall during a strike. Once these have been calculated they can be used to calculate the net benefits from a strike and if these are positive a strike will ensue.

Turning to the position of the trade union leader, it is probable that up to a point he will be willing to agree to a negotiation wage less than his target wage rather than incur a strike. Exactly how far he will be prepared to lower his demands will again depend upon the expected relative gains and losses from incurring a strike. The gains now relate to the increase in the negotiated wage which he can expect the strike to bring about. More exactly they equal the increased proportion of his membership who find it acceptable. In addition, as we noted before, there may be an impact effect from the strike on the permanent income calculations which reduces the individual's aspiration wages. This may bring them down to more realistic levels, thus reducing the dissatisfaction with the negotiated wage from the level it would have been in the absence of a strike. The union leader can also hope for increased support for and understanding of his position now that he is seen to be in direct conflict with the employer in the workers' interests. As with the employer these benefits may not just relate to the workers involved in a particular negotiation. The union may take the view that the negotiated wage may set a pattern for other negotiations in which the union is involved.

The potential costs of a strike may be measured by any dissatisfaction on the part of some of the membership concerning the strike. It may be that although the best wage offer that could be secured in the absence of a strike does not satisfy as high a proportion of the membership as the union leader might wish, it does satisfy some. This section of the membership may not then wish to strike and may become dissatisfied with the leadership. There is also a risk of other workers becoming dissatisfied, if, for example, the increase in the negotiated wage brought about by the strike seems insufficient to compensate for income forgone during the strike. The trade union leader must also consider a different kind of cost, not concerning increased dissatisfaction with him by the membership, but a reduction in the size of that membership. This may occur if the increased cost of labour encourages employers to use a more capital intensive mode of production resulting in a reduced labour force. It may also be possible in some cases that the wage increase makes some employers so uncompetitive that it forces them to close down altogether. These effects are likely to be more important when there is some slack in the economy. A reduction in demand for the firm's products is then more likely following a price rise, and redundant workers will have increased difficulty in finding work.

The union leader will then be faced with the same type of dual decision problem as the employer. First he must calculate the expected duration of the strike, and from this the increase in the negotiated wage he can expect the strike to bring about. Besides the factors already discussed these will also depend on the speed with which the union leader expects the negotiated wage to fall throughout the duration of the strike. Once these have been calculated they can be used to calculate the net benefits from a strike, and if they are positive a strike will ensue.

Comparing now the positions of the employer and union leader we can see that if the minimum wage the union leader will accept is less than the maximum one to which the employer will agree, then there will be no strike. The negotiated wage will then lie somewhere between these two limits; exactly where will depend upon the relative bargaining skills of the two sides. If, however, the minimum wage the union leader is willing to agree to is in excess of the maximum one to which the employer will agree there will be a strike. With the onset of a strike we can expect some immediate changes in the bargaining positions of the two sides. It may be that there will be a reduction in the wage that the union leader will be willing to accept, following an immediate impact effect on his membership's permanent income calculations. In addition, with the onset of a strike the dissatisfaction of any workers who were satisfied with the employer's last offer, and therefore did not want to strike, will become more voluble. Similarly, for the employer we might expect to see some increase in the wage to which he is willing to agree as potential dissatisfaction from customers who have had their supplies cut off becomes more voluble. On the other hand, it might be that both union leader and employer will have anticipated such reactions. Significant changes in their bargaining position might not then occur until there is some indication that original expectations concerning the duration of the strike were too optimistic. The winner in this confrontation will be the side who can adopt the most convincing hard line stance. The union may have increasing difficulties in maintaining a united position on the strike amongst its membership. The employer will be concerned with the continued loss of profits, and perhaps increasingly about a possible permanent loss of custom.

Summary

This chapter has sought to develop a synthesis between excess demand theories of inflation and wage bargaining ones. Hitherto these two approaches to wage inflation have generally been regarded as being mutually exclusive, with the acceptance of one precluding the acceptance of the other. However, it seems to me that both contain essential insights which the other ignores. Therefore by combining these two theories together we can obtain a more complete understanding of the inflationary process.

We began this synthesis by developing a search theoretic approach to the employer's side of the problem. This differed from previous search theories in several respects. In practice it stressed the effects of economic conditions on search productivity, which most other theories have ignored, generally assuming that each period will produce one interview. The assumption of constant search productivity is the basis for two of the criticisms that have been levelled at search theories, these being, first, that they make all unemployment search unemployment, which is synonymous with voluntary unemployment, and secondly that variations in the unemployment rate only occur because someone is being fooled, makes a false prediction or lacks all the relevant information. In the model we have developed all unemployment remains search unemployment, but only in the sense that all the unemployed are searching for a job. This is voluntary only in the sense that no acceptable offer has yet been found, which includes both the case where the searcher has a high reservation wage, and where job market conditions are such that interviews are difficult to find. Yet only the first of these could conceivably be called voluntary, and even then the dividing line between what is and is not voluntary is so hazy that it is probably best to dispense with the term altogether. Also, within the context of the theory, changes in unemployment can occur for reasons other than job searchers being overly optimistic or unduly pessimistic. In particular we could expect to see a change in unemployment if the productivity of search for the employer or employee changes. If, for example, there is an increase in vacancies we can expect, in the long run, a fall in unemployment as job searchers obtain more interviews per period.

However, even though we have gone some way in meeting some of the criticisms which have been levelled at search theories, others remain. Chief amongst these is the assumption that only unemployed workers engage in search activity, on the job search being ruled out. The justification for simplifying assumptions is that they allow us to model complex real life situations, and thereby gain insights that were not previously apparent. Several such insights have emerged from this theory, including the concept of backlogs of quits and fires as labour market conditions change, the role of profits within an excess demand framework, and the possibility of a non-unit variable coefficient on expectations.

Hitherto profits have largely been ignored within an excess demand framework, although they have received some attention in bargaining models. This lack of interest may in part be due to the influence of an early paper by Lipsey and Steur (1961) who found only a weak relationship between wage changes and profits in the UK. However, it should be noted that they used the level of profits corrected for price changes, but not for real secular growth in the economy. This is important, for an increase in profits due, for example, to an increase in output resulting from an expansion of the labour force, is not likely to have any effect on wage inflation. We should also note that it is not simply the level of profits that is relevant, but rather the net revenue contribution per worker. This is related to profits, but due to productivity growth, given a constant level of profits, we should expect this to increase over time, with the simple Phillips curve type relation also shifting outwards.

The possibility of a non-unit coefficient on expectations arises because a unit coefficient will only serve to maintain an absolute differential over the wages an employer expects others to be paying. To maintain a relative differential, which I feel is more in keeping with both the logic and spirit of search theories, the coefficient on expectations must vary with labour market conditions.

We then examined the implications of further considering the lessons from implicit contract theory. On the basis of these it was argued that the employer would take into account the effect of the wage he pays on his reputation as a fair employer. A fair wage was defined to be one that would enable the individual worker to just maintain his planned consumption stream, based on permanent income considerations. If the wage the employer would wish to pay on pure search theoretic considerations exceeds this fair wage, then this will be the wage the employer pays. If it does not then the fair wage becomes a more active consideration. The employer is unlikely to pay the fair wage in full. He will trade off the advantages of doing so, in terms of his reputation, against the costs, which are of course the increase in his wage bill. Once an employer enters into negotiations with a trade union, the differing wages he would like to pay each individual worker coalesce into one common wage he wishes to negotiate with the union leader, called the employer's competitive wage. This is a significant departure from previous bargaining theories which assumed that the employer would merely attempt to negotiate as low a wage as possible.

Having examined the employer's side of the bargaining problem, we turned to that of the trade union. Building on a theoretical base developed by Ross and Ashenfelter and Johnson, we analysed the interactions between the union leader and his membership. It was suggested that the principal aim of the union leader was to retain his job, and that he could best do this by satisfying the aspirations of some minimum proportion of his membership. The worker's aspiration wage in this respect is none other than the fair wage we have just discussed. To repeat the definition, it is the wage which just allows him to maintain his standard of living in the form of his planned consumption stream. Out of such considerations emerges a wage rate that the union leader wants to secure in the negotiations, his target wage.

If the employer's competitive wage exceeds the union leader's target wage, then this is the wage that will be negotiated. If, however, this is not the case then we are in a more genuine bargaining situation. Both sides will be willing to compromise on their original negotiating positions, in order to prevent a strike. The union leader in particular may make tactical calculations about the most opportune time to strike, not attempting to fully satisfy his membership's aspirations in each contract, but only on average over time, perhaps judging that a threat to his position will develop only if he repeatedly fails to secure adequate increases. If the minimum wage a trade union leader is willing to accept is less than the maximum one that the employer is willing to offer, then agreement will be reached without a strike. If not the wage eventually negotiated will still lie between the union leader's target wage and the employer's competitive wage, although the latter wage may have changed as a result of the strike, as the employer will probably have then lost his reputation for fairness.

The relevance of this for inflation is easy to see. Defining the competitive wage and the target wage as averages across employers and union leaders, a practice we shall follow from now on, we can see that when the competitive wage exceeds the target wage, wages and wage inflation will largely be determined by search theoretic considerations which give rise to the Phillips curve. When this is not the case, when the target wage exceeds the competitive wage, then we are in a more genuine bargaining situation, search considerations will not be nearly so important, and the Phillips curve ceases to be a valid approximation.

We shall later be considering how well this theory can explain events both in the USA and the UK, after which we shall turn briefly to examine the policy implications of the theory, again with specific reference to these two countries. Before doing that, however, we shall examine how expectations are formed. As we have seen these play a crucial role in my, as well as other, theories of inflation.

Chapter 3

Expectations of Inflation

Expectations as a concept seem to be growing increasingly important, and much of economic theory is now being rewritten to take explicit account of them. Indeed in future years when economists look back at this era, it may well prove to be that this is seen as the thread that links together much of the work being done, as in a similar manner the rejection of the assumption of perfect knowledge characterises much of the work done in the interwar period. However, this awareness of the importance of expectations is not a new phenomenon. Marshall (1920), for example, was aware of the importance of the concept, although as Shackle (1967) comments, this was not a trumpet he chose to blow too hard. But it was really in Sweden that the importance of expectations in economic theory was first fully appreciated, with the work of Myrdal (1939), amongst others, while in England at about this time Keynes' General Theory had just appeared, in which expectations are of prime importance.

Most of this early work was connected with the effects of expectations, rather than with how they were formed. Keynes, at least, thought that some expectations were closely akin to a random variable, and hence unexplainable, that is, unless a theory of animal spirits can be provided. Since then, and particularly since 1960, a substantial volume of literature has appeared concerned with how expectations are formed. This can be divided into two fairly distinct parts, that dealing with theoretical considerations, and that which is mainly empirical in nature. There has, of course, been some interchange between these two avenues of research, but unfortunately this has not been common, and they have by and large remained separate areas. It is hoped in this survey not only to summarise these two approaches, but to forge closer links between them.

Theories of Expectation Formation

One of the first studies to put forward a hypothesis of expectation formation was Exekial's study of the cobweb theorem (1938). He assumed expectations were formed in a 'naive' manner, that is, the expected price was equal to the most recently known price, although if it were being put forward today it would probably relate not to the price level, but to its rate of change. A slightly more sophisticated model was proposed by Hicks (1946), and is known as the extrapolative expectations hypothesis. It can be written as

$$\dot{P}_t^e = a_0 + a_1\dot{P}_t + a_2(\dot{P}_t - \dot{P}_{t-1}) \qquad (3.1)$$

Hicks assumed that $a_0 = 0$ and $a_1 = 1$, but an alternative version proposed by Metzler (1941) allowed these parameters to take alternative values. Hicks's original model asserted that the expected rate of inflation equals the current inflation rate plus an adjustment factor which allows for the rate of change of inflation. In other words people are forming their expectations not simply about the rate of inflation, but also the rate of change of that. This is basically a second order expectations mechanism, and as such seems rather over-sophisticated for times of normal inflation. Since Hicks wrote the term, extrapolative hypothesis has been used to describe any method of expectation formation which is based upon a distributed lag of actual prices, that is,

$$\dot{P}_t^e = \sum a_i\dot{P}_{t-i} \qquad (3.2)$$

In this form it is probably more acceptable than Hicks's formation, which it includes as a special case.

A third approach to expectation formation, which can also be viewed as a special case of the extrapolative hypothesis, has come to dominate much of the work done on expectations. This is the adaptive expectations hypothesis, first put forward by Cagan (1956) and Nerlove (1958). It states that expectations are revised in accordance with the last forecasting error; hence its alternative name, the error learning hypothesis. Algebraically it can be expressed as

$$\dot{P}_t^e = \lambda\dot{P}_t + (1-\lambda)\dot{P}_{t-1}^e \qquad (3.3)$$

which is equivalent to an extrapolative model with geometrically declining weights:

$$\dot{P}_t^e = \lambda \sum_{i=0}^{\infty} (1-\lambda)^i\dot{P}_{t-i} \qquad (3.4)$$

λ is the adjustment parameter and the larger it is the more rapid is the adjustment of expectations to the actual rate of inflation, or alternatively the more rapid the weights decline in (3.4).

Another variation of the extrapolative theme, which has received some prominence recently, is the regressive–extrapolative expectations hypothesis. This was first put forward by Duesenberry (1958), and expanded upon by Modigliani and Sutch (1966). They suggest that there might be both extrapolative and regressive elements present in the process by which expectations are formed. The latter implies a reversion of expectations towards a long-run 'normal' level, which may in itself be a given parameter of the system, or a lagged function of actual price changes, where the lag may extend over several years. In the latter case the hypothesis once more becomes a special case of the general extrapolative hypothesis.

There is one further major theory of expectation formation. This is, of course, the rational expectations hypothesis. This differs from the other hypotheses we have mentioned in that expectations of price inflation are not based on the present and past behaviour of prices. It was originally proposed by Muth (1961), who argued that expectations are formed in accordance with the 'relevant economic theory'. In Muth's own words (p. 315):

In particular the hypothesis asserts that the economy does not waste information and that expectations depend specifically on the structure of the entire system.

In more formal terms the rational expectations hypothesis proposes that expectations, or more generally the subjective probability distribution of outcomes, tends to be distributed, for the same information set, about the prediction of the theory.

These are the major theories of expectation formation. However, some economists, for example, Carlson and Parkin (1975), have suggested that actual expectation formation does not correspond to any single one of these by itself. Rather elements from several theories may be relevant in the formation of expectations. Thus we have, for example, the rational–adaptive hypothesis, whereby expectations are formed partly by an adaptive mechanism and partly by taking into account non-price information, in a rational manner.

How does one decide between these differing theories? There have been two approaches. The first examines theoretical considerations, and the second looks at the empirical evidence. We shall develop the theoretical approach first.

A Theoretical Evaluation of the Differing Theories

The majority of the work aimed at providing a theoretical justification for any of these hypotheses has been couched in terms of optimal forecasting considerations, the exceptions to this being papers by Turnovsky (1969) and Cyert and DeGroot (1974), who both adopt a Bayesian framework for their analyses. These two papers, although they develop a different approach to the rest of the literature, also parallel it in one important respect. They concentrate on the adaptive and rational expectations hypotheses. We will begin this part of the survey with these two papers. This order of approach is not based upon chronological considerations. It merely reflects the fact that these two papers do not fit in well with the rest of the literature, and it was decided to deal with them at the beginning rather than at the end of the survey.

Turnovsky's paper shows that if we can regard expectations as being altered in a Bayesian manner over time and the prior distribution is normal, then expectations for period $t + 1$, formed at period t, can be obtained from the following equation

$$P_t^e - P_{t-1}^e = (1 - W_t/W_{t-1})(P_t - P_{t-1}^e) \qquad (3.5)$$

where W_t is the variance of the distribution of expected prices and P_t^e is the mean of that distribution. This is very similar to the adaptive expectations hypothesis with the coefficient of adaption, λ, being equal to the first term in parentheses on the right-hand side of (3.5). It differs, however, in that this is not constant over time. This is because W_t declines as the individual's knowledge of the system increases. The change in W_t will become smaller as it approaches zero which will in turn reduce the coefficient of adaption. In the limit expectations will be constant.

Turnovsky's paper is interesting in as much as it shows how the parameters may be arrived at within an adaptive expectations mechanism. But its more general relevance is limited by the fact that it takes as a basis a time series which is generated by random fluctuations around a given mean. The decision maker's problem is then to find that mean. Given more observations he will become more and more confident in his estimate and respond less and less to temporary fluctuations. The problem faced by real world decision makers, at least with regard to forecasting future inflation rates, is generally more complex. More realistic analyses can be built around variants of an integrated autoregressive moving average (ARIMA) process with which the remainder of the literature has been primarily concerned, and which seem more capable of generating time series similar to those we observe in the real world.

Cyert and DeGroot also develop a Bayesian analysis, but to describe the process by which rational expectations may be developed within a market clearing model of supply and demand, the model they take is essentially the one Muth used to illustrate the concept of rational expectations, which we shall discuss later. Their version of Muth's three-equation model is

$$C_t = d_1 - \beta P_t \qquad \text{(demand)} \qquad (3.6a)$$

$$Q_t = d_2 + \gamma P^e_{t-1} + U_t \qquad \text{(supply)} \qquad (3.6b)$$

$$Q_t = C_t \qquad \text{(market equilibrium)} \qquad (3.6c)$$

where d_1 and d_2 are parameters and U_t a random disturbance term. By solving the market equations we get

$$P_t = \frac{d_1 - d_2}{\beta} - \frac{\gamma}{\beta}P^e_{t-1} - \frac{1}{\beta}U_t \qquad (3.7)$$

Then, assuming that each U_t has a normal distribution with zero mean and known precision, they show that, where P^e_t is equivalent to the mathematical definition of the expected value of P_t,

$$\plim_{t \to \infty} P^e_t = \frac{(d_1 - d_2)}{\beta + \gamma} \qquad (3.8)$$

The main weakness in this result is again its lack of generality. The problem here has been to estimate constant parameter values within a model. In the more general case the rational expectations hypothesis supposes that certain variables depend upon the values of certain other variables, and Cyert and DeGroot have little to say about this relationship. Indeed, in as much as we can regard the rational expectations hypothesis as having an extrapolative basis (a statement we shall expand upon later), it would seem that Turnovsky's work has more relevance for the rational expectations hypothesis.

The remainder of this literature has been mainly concerned with optimal forecasting considerations. The basis for this approach was again laid by Muth (1960). In this paper he showed that if a time series can be regarded as following the process shown below

$$Y_t = \epsilon_t + \beta \sum_{i=1} \epsilon_{t-i} \qquad (3.9)$$

where

$$E(\epsilon_t) = 0, \quad \text{var}(\epsilon_t) = \sigma^2 \quad \text{and} \quad 0 < \beta < 1$$

then an adaptive expectations measure of expectations is optimal, the adaptive expectations coefficient being equal to β. The time series in (3.9) corresponds to a linear function of random shocks, where the shock associated with each period has a weight of unity. Its weight in successive time periods is then constant and lies somewhere between zero and one.

He also shows that the same type of forecasting rule is optimal if the time series approximates a random walk with noise superimposed, that is,

$$Y_t = \sum_{i=0}^{\infty} \epsilon_{t-i} + \eta_t \qquad (3.10)$$

Important in all this literature is the criterion of optimality employed and here again Muth set the pattern which most succeeding studies were to follow. His criterion was that of minimum variance, that is, the optimal forecasting method is the one that minimises the variance of the forecast error. The criterion used has obvious implications for the conclusions reached as to the optimal forecasting mechanism, and later we shall consider the specific implications of choosing a minimum variance criterion.

The time series considered by Muth are rather limited in character and some work has been done to extend his results to cover the more general cases. This work has been partially summarised by Rose (1972), who examines the optimal forecasting method when the time series can be regarded as an ARIMA process. The principal conclusion is that the optimal current period forecast will, in general, be a weighted average of n previous errors, where n will depend upon the exact properties of the time series to be forecast. The adaptive expectations mechanism is then only optimal when $n = 1$.

A simple ARMA process of order (p,q) is a combination of p autoregressive and q moving average terms, for example, when $p = 2$ and $q = 3$ we have

$$Y_t = p_1 Y_{t-1} + p_2 Y_{t-2} + a + e_t + q_1 e_{t-1} + q_2 e_{t-2} + q_3 e_{t-3}$$

$$(3.11)$$

An ARIMA (p, d, q) process is then simply an ARMA process stationary not in terms of Y, but in the dth difference in Y.

If the time series we are interested in can be described by such a process, the optimal forecast, in terms of minimising the error variance, is as we have already said a weighted average of n previous errors, where n will depend upon the characteristics of the ARIMA process.

An alternative way of looking at the problem of expectation formation, which is useful for the different perspective it gives to the problem, is provided by regarding it as a special application of the Kalman filter. Given a model

$$y_t = A_t y_{t-1} + C_t x_t + b_t + u_t \qquad (3.12)$$

where lower case letters denote vectors and upper case letters denote matrices, y_{t-1} is a vector of lagged dependent variables and x_t a vector of exogenous variables. We do not observe y_t directly, only its observational equivalent, s_t, related to y_t by the observation equation

$$s_t = M_t y_t + \eta_t \qquad (3.13)$$

where the disturbance terms have the usual properties and M_t is a known matrix. The problem is to find the mean vector y_t given the observational equivalent s_t. Applying the Kalman filter gives

$$E(y_t|s_t) = (I - D_t M_t)(A_t E(y_{t-1}|s_{t-1}) + C_t x_t + b_t) + D_t s_t$$
$$(3.14)$$

where D_t is a matrix of revision coefficients corresponding to the updating of expectations of y_t given the new observation matrix s_t, that is,

$$E(y_t|s_t) = E(y_t|s_{t-1}) + D_t(s_t - E(s_t|s_{t-1})) \qquad (3.15)$$

Equation (3.14) gives the principal result of the Kalman filter and has been used extensively, particularly in engineering. It was derived as a conditional expectation of y_t given s_t. As such it is an optimal estimator of y_t, in the sense of being a minimum variance estimator. It was originally put forward by Kalman (1960) in rather a difficult paper. A somewhat simpler exposition can be found in Chow (1975).

Its relevance to the adaptive expectations hypothesis was first made explicit by L. Taylor (1970) and Nerlove (1972). For this y_t is reduced to a single dependent variable and (3.12) becomes

$$y_t = a y_{t-1} + u_t \qquad (3.16)$$

The filtering equation (3.15) now becomes

$$E(y_t|s_t) = (1 - d_t)a(E(y_{t-1}|s_{t-1})) + d_t s_t \qquad (3.17)$$

This mention of the Kalman filter is interesting in several respects.

First, some economic analyses of expectations seem unaware of it, but it should be of some interest to those concerned with the development of economic ideas. Secondly, this alternative way of looking at expectations, as being essentially the filtering of a permanent element from a time series, emphasises something which underlies most theories of expectation formation, but is often not made explicit, namely, that we regard the time series as consisting of permanent and temporary elements, and in some way it is this permanent element that we are trying to isolate. Finally, the Kalman filter provides a justification for the adaptive expectations hypothesis using a different rationale than Muth's.

Taken together these results do seem to provide some justification for the hypothesis that expectations are based upon the past behaviour of the forecast variable. However, this conclusion is not without its qualifications. Nelson (1975) shows that if a variable can be regarded as being endogenously determined within an economic model, then, in general, rational expectations based upon that model will provide optimal forecasts, and not expectations based upon the past behaviour of that variable. In particular this is the case even when the variable can be specified as a linear function of random disturbance terms. For example, consider a structure with only two inputs

$$x_t = \sum_{i=0}^{\infty} \psi_i u_{t-i} \quad \text{and} \quad y_t = \sum_{i=0}^{\infty} \theta_i v_{t-i} \qquad (3.18)$$

where

$$z_t = x_t + y_t$$

$$= \sum_{i=0}^{\infty} \psi_i u_{t-i} + \sum_{i=0}^{\infty} \theta_i v_{t-i} \qquad (3.19)$$

we could then write z_t as a linear function of its own past history

$$z_t = \sum_{i=0}^{\infty} \pi_i w_{t-i} \qquad (3.20)$$

where w_t is a sequence of uncorrelated disturbances with variance σ_w^2. This follows from Wold's decomposition theory. Since x_t and y_t are both stationary and independent, z_t must also be stationary and can be expressed as a linear stochastic process of the form (which is equivalent to (3.20))

$$z_t = \sum_{i=1}^{\infty} \lambda_i z_{t-i} + w_t \qquad (3.21)$$

Thus both rational expectations, based on (3.19), and extrapolative expectations, based on (3.21), may be formed, although it should be noted that the rational mechanism consists of first forming expectations about x_t and y_t and then using these to predict z_t. This first set of expectations are themselves formed in an extrapolative manner. It was the gist of Nelson's paper that this procedure would give a smaller mean square prediction error than extrapolative expectations based on (3.21).

This result has since been generalised by Wallis (1980) to cover all cases where the exogenous variables in the model follow an ARIMA process. This would seem to be the *coup de grâce*, and indeed in the context of the ground rules within which the debate has been conducted it is. If one accepts that the criteria of optimality must be based solely upon minimising the error variance, then we must conclude that wherever such a model is applicable expectations must be formed in accordance with that model. However, if we return to Muth's original paper (Muth, 1961) we see that one of the principal justifications for his hypothesis was (p. 330):

> If expectations were not moderately rational there would be opportunities for economists to make profits in commodity speculation, running a firm or selling the information to the present owners.

Yet we now observe this last phenomenon. Economists are now employed by private agencies to formulate forecasts which are sold to firms. This would therefore seem to weaken the foundations upon which the rational expectations hypothesis is built. This conclusion is even more justified if we consider how professional economic forecasters arrive at their forecasts. Do they take advantage of modern computer technology to construct full scale economic models, the parameters of which are estimated by regression techniques? Unfortunately, they do not. In general, forecasts are based upon extrapolative models, for example, Box–Jenkins models which have come into vogue in recent years.

There are several possible reasons as to why they do this, Nelson himself suggested one important possibility (Nelson, 1975, p. 343):

> Of course unlike the hypothetical rational economic agent who knows the parameters as well as the form of the economic structure he deals with, econometric models may be subject to errors of specification and parameter estimation. We can only speculate that these errors are great enough at the present state of the art to prevent structural models from attaining their potential as tools of prediction.

What Nelson seems to be saying here is that the superiority of rational over extrapolative forecasts is only valid as long as all the parameters are known with certainty and that they relate to the correct economic model which is also known. If this is not the case then he seems to be saying that the issue is undecided. However, the very fact that professional forecasters use an extrapolative model would seem to suggest that for many time series this both now and presumably in the past also represents the optimal model to use in forecasting the future.

A second consideration is that of the time profile of the availability of the data. In the simple model described by equation (3.19), for example, it may be that z_t is known sooner than x_t or y_t. In this case, even with complete information about parameter values, the extrapolative scheme based upon more up to date information might provide better estimates than those based upon rational expectations.

A further problem with the rational expectations hypothesis is just how individuals obtain their knowledge of the economic system, its structure and parameter values. Unfortunately this has only been partially dealt with in the literature. Some consideration has been given as to how individuals might obtain estimates of the parameters, generally within a least squares or Bayesian framework. Thus Blanchard (1976) used a discrete time model to investigate the problem of how agents discover the correct specification of the model generating the behaviour of the overall system. His results showed that even given an infinite amount of time in which to learn, agents' beliefs about the specification will not necessarily converge to that of the true model. So expectations will not necessarily become rational in Muth's sense. Taylor (1975) used a continuous time model in which agents already know all aspects of the system except the value of a single parameter in the (correctly) specified equation, describing the behaviour of the monetary policy authority. In this case estimates of the parameter did converge to the true value.

Both these examples are based on extremely simplistic situations. More relevant is the question of how individuals, uncertain as to the exact economic structure as well as the parameter values, obtain that information. Moreover, even if we could assume that they do, the further question remains as to what characterises their expectations during the learning process. This latter question has been considered by B. Friedman (1979), who concludes that it is extremely unlikely that expectations in the past could have been rational in Muth's sense. A particular problem is the many drastic changes that have taken place in economists' views as to the underlying process which generates inflation.

An Evaluation of the Optimality Criteria

Hitherto only one type of cost has been considered, that of the expectations being in error, and in general this has been considered within only one context, the error variance, thus implicitly assuming that expectation formation is a costless activity. This assumption has been recently questioned by Feige and Pearce (1976) who introduce the concept of 'economically rational' expectations for a world in which information costs are non-trivial. This emphasises that an economic agent should consider the trade-off between the benefits and the costs of added information, where the benefits relate to the increased accuracy of the forecasts. This approach helps us to explain why individuals do not form expectations on all possible time series, why, for example, non-car owners are unlikely to form expectations about petrol prices. This kind of behaviour is incapable of being explained by the standard approach, which has nothing to say about which variables individuals will form expectations about and which they will ignore. However, the modified cost function approach tells us that individuals will not form expectations for those series where the total costs of the optimal method of expectation formation exceed the benefits of those expectations.

Thus, in reaching a conclusion about optimal methods of expectation formation two points should be borne in mind: the formation costs of any particular method and its accuracy. Moreover, for methods where parameter values have to be learned over a period of time, the transition costs should also be borne in mind. These transition costs will consist partly of the increased error in forecasts as the individual learns about the model, both its structure and parameters. Thus it will not always be the case that the most accurate method, that is, the minimum variance one, will be optimal, for it may well be that this also involves heavy formation costs. The great advantage of the adaptive expectations hypothesis lies in its simplicity, and hence in its relatively small formation costs. Knowledge is only required of the current value of the time series being forecast and a single parameter. Compare this with the large number of parameters and variables which must be used in calculations using extrapolative, large order error learning and rational schemes, and we have perhaps a major reason for its popularity amongst many economists. Such considerations may also explain why professional forecasters tend to use extrapolative methods rather than building full scale econometric models.

These two hypotheses have so far been put forward as competing theories, and indeed this is largely how they have been approached within the literature. Yet, as often happens, this has served to obscure how much common ground there exists between the rational expectations hypothesis and the various extrapolative theories. The rational expectations hypothesis as propounded so far is not, in general terms, an alternative to extrapolative theories. It cannot be for it is often based upon extrapolative expectations. This is, as we have already made clear, the case for the rational expectations scheme described in equation (3.19). Thus the rational expectations hypothesis in this form seems to be suggesting that some expectations are formed rationally and some extrapolatively, in which case the real debate should be concerned with which variables come into which category, rather than trying to establish the superiority of one of these two methods of expectation formation for all expectations.

Few economists would deny that some expectations are formed rationally although the theory probably has most relevance in the context within which Muth originally placed it — the decision making process of the firm. However, there may well be other areas of decision making where it has some relevance. But with respect to the theory of inflation, the most important set of expectations relate to future wage and price levels held by employer and employee. We are now far removed from the simple, single good, supply and demand context within which Muth first introduced his hypothesis. The most striking difference is that there is no universally accepted model of inflation. What we do have are a number of competing theories, none of which are capable of explaining the inflationary process in a satisfactory manner. For any economist to assume that such expectations are formed in accordance with the particular theory he favours seems completely unjustifiable, even more so when they call for working men to have a detailed knowledge of the money supply and how it interacts with the price level.

However, it would seem almost as unlikely that individuals base their expectations upon a pure extrapolative scheme. One cannot dismiss Tobin's (1972) claim — that people obtain information about the economic system through newspapers — that easily. The media is important, and when the public read or hear of a forthcoming prices and incomes policy, a currency devaluation, or an oil price rise, then it seems likely that they will use this information in forming their expectations. But Tobin's observation, in order to be taken as a justification for the rational expectations hypothesis, must be supplemented by two further assumptions. First, the newspapers, and this means basically the tabloids, television and radio, need to give regular price forecasts based upon the 'relevant theory', and secondly these need to be perceived and believed by the working population as a whole. Neither of these propositions seems likely to be true. What seems more likely is that expectations are formed in a semi-rational, semi-extrapolative manner – the rational–extrapolative hypothesis, as suggested by Carlson and Parkin, whereby expectations are formed primarily in an extrapolative manner, by which we mean the adaptive expectations mechanism, but outside factors such as those already mentioned might also have an effect.

We conclude this section by foreshadowing a conclusion which we might make in more definite terms at a later stage in the analysis. For applied economists it is not an encouraging conclusion, but it seems inescapable. The problem of modelling peoples' expectations is an extremely difficult one, and it does not seem probable that any one mechanism is used all the time. The most likely combination is the rational–extrapolative one, with the weights of the different components differing with time. It may be that the rational component is increasing with time as the general public becomes economically more literate. It may also be that the parameters within the extrapolative element vary with time, so that in some periods a more complex scheme is used than at others. But exactly when these changes take place, and how people take account of external information such as commodity/raw material price rises, devaluation, etc., is not obvious. This implies that it is going to be very difficult to generate an accurate series of expectations for use in time series analyses. Nor can we easily get round the problem by trying to include the expectation formation process within the structure of the model. But the attempt must be made. If theoretical considerations lead us to believe that expectations are an important explanatory variable, then they somehow must be proxied.

Empirical Evidence on Expectation Formation

Empirical work on expectation formation has proceeded in two general directions. The first uses actual data on expectations, while the second includes the expectation mechanism within the structure of the model being estimated. We shall concentrate on the first of these two methods, before turning briefly to examine the second.

Direct tests on the formation of expectations have been comparatively limited. This is principally because of the difficulty in obtaining data on expectations. There have again been two general methods of proceeding. The first is to obtain data directly from sample surveys. The second derives the data indirectly by observing the consequences of peoples' behaviour when expectations enter the decision making process. In practice this generally implies observing the difference between price indexed and non-price indexed bonds.

One of the first studies to use survey data was Turnovsky's (1970). He derived the data from the Livingstone survey of business and academic economists in the USA. This is a bi-annual survey that seeks predictions for a number of economic series, including the consumer price index. Using these data Turnovsky found that there appeared to be a change in behaviour around 1963–4. Prior to this neither the adaptive expectations nor the extrapolative hypotheses worked very well. Expectations appeared to be constant with some correction being made for past trends, which businessmen tended to extrapolate. However, in the later period both adaptive and extrapolative models fared better by the standard statistical measures. In addition, the sum of the two coefficients in the adaptive expectations model was not significantly different from 1. The coefficient of adaption itself was approximately 0.78, which suggests rapid adjustment of expectations to the rate of inflation. However, it should be noted that he was forced, by the nature of the data, to assume that expectations are revised at six-monthly intervals, and it is possible that if expectations are revised more frequently, the adjustment coefficient will be biased. This is a point to which we shall return later. Finally it should be noted that he included the rate of unemployment in the regressions, but this was not significant.

Turnovsky also used the Livingstone data in a second study, this time in conjunction with Wachter (1972), in which they tested extrapolative, adaptive and rational theories of expectation formation. The results are shown in Table 3.1 and suggest that in this case rational expectations furnish a superior explanation of expectation formation than simple adaptive or extrapolative schemes. The particular model proposed is a simple price expectations augmented Phillips curve, with wage inflation as the independent variable. The most plausible explanation for the two unemployment variables is that both the level of unemployment and its rate of change are considered within the rational model.

However, in evaluating these results it should be borne in mind that there are a number of shortcomings with the data. These have been analysed in a paper by Carlson (1977) who points out that the data collected by Livingstone relate to price levels, and that it is from these that the expected inflation rates are derived. The main difficulty with this is that the predictions are made for June and December, that is, six months after they are published. But the predictions are not made in the months they are published, but in the previous ones, that is, in November and May. Moreover the latest data available in those months relates to the previous months, that is, October and April. He also notes that when the price index given to the respondents changes between the survey date and the

Table 3.1   *Turnovsky and Wachter's results*

Model	Equations	R^2	DW
Extrapolative	$\dot{W}_t^e = 0.809\dot{W}_t - 0.318(\dot{W}_t - \dot{W}_{t-1})$ $\quad\quad(9.566)\quad\ (2.293)$	0.148	1.12
Adaptive	$\dot{W}_t^e = 0.533\dot{W}_t + 0.337\dot{W}_{t-1}^e$ $\quad\quad(4.896)\quad\ (2.798)$	0.242	1.86
Rational	$\dot{W}_t^e = 1.531 + 33.617U_t^{-1}$ $\quad\quad(1.262)\ (3.493)$ $\quad\quad\quad - 30.713U_{t-1}^{-1} + 0.503\dot{P}_t$ $\quad\quad\quad\ (3.335)\quad\quad\quad (3.256)$	0.490	1.59
Rational	$\dot{W}_t^e = 1.185 + 28.880U_t^{-1}$ $\quad\quad(1.009)\ (2.985)$ $\quad\quad\quad - 23.273U_{t-1}^{-1} + 0.624\dot{P}_t^e$ $\quad\quad\quad\ (2.440)\quad\quad\quad (3.76)$	0.527	2.14

Notes: The expectations are revised bi-annually and are for six months ahead. They relate to the period 1949–69. The numbers in parentheses are t statistics.

publication date, Livingstone sometimes adjusts the forecasts to allow for this additional information. Carlson argues that this is not done consistently or accurately enough and introduces measurement errors into the data. He then readjusts the series to bring the data closer to their original form and argues that they should correctly be used to calculate eight and fourteen month forecasts, instead of the six and twelve month forecasts as interpreted by Turnovsky.

But the chief qualification to these results must be that they are formed by business and academic economists, and therefore they may not be representative of the way the population as a whole form their expectations. This is important, for economists are much more likely to form their expectations in accordance with the relevant economic theory than the rest of the population. In addition, Livingstone provides the respondents with up to date information about the economy, and therefore the problem of how people perceive this information is not tackled. These considerations impose serious limitations on the results. Yet they do not render them completely invalid, and it seems possible that several of the characteristics of these expectations might be carried over to expectations in general.

For example, the relative insensitivity of these expectations to actual price changes between the end of the Korean War and 1965 may reflect a lack of concern with price changes by the population as a whole during this period. Within the theory developed in the previous section this could be explained by the total cost of the optimal expectations mechanism exceeding the costs of remaining ignorant about future price trends. Hence no expectations are formed at all, or alternatively a constant expectation is held. The second characteristic which we might bear in mind for future discussion is that typically the expectations appear to underestimate the actual price change during periods of unusually high inflation, such as the Korean War or the early 1970s.

Carlson and Parkin (1975) were faced with a different set of problems from those trying to use the Livingstone data. They had qualitative data for the UK, on a monthly basis for the period 1961–73. The data were obtained from Gallup poll surveys of approximately 1000 quota sampled individuals who were asked whether they expected prices to rise, fall or stay the same. The principal problem that Carlson and Parkin were faced with was how to convert this data into a quantitative form that would be more amenable to economic analysis. In solving this they made a number of assumptions, most of which were related to the distribution of expectations across individuals, a slightly unusual one being that there is a range of price changes about zero which the respondent cannot distinguish from zero. This range of imperceptibility is what experimental psychologists have called the difference limen, and is defined as the increase in physical stimulus just necessary to produce a noticeable difference in sensation. Having derived a quantitative data series on expectations they then used it to test several versions of the adaptive expectations hypothesis. A simple first order adaptive expectations mechanism, with an added dummy variable to represent the effects of the 1967 devaluation of the pound, gave generally good results, although the coefficients on current inflation and lagged expectations summed to only 0.877 as opposed to their theoretical value of unity. The remaining regressions all tested a second order error learning mechanism, which the authors suggest could be appropriate if people took account not only of the current recent rate of inflation, but also its rate of change. They found that prior to 1967, when inflation was low, a simple autoregressive scheme seemed appropriate, but that after that something approaching a second order learning mechanism fitted the data better.

One can question their interpretation of a second order learning mechanism, as defined below

$$\dot{P}_t^e = \lambda_1 \dot{P}_t + (1 - \lambda_1)\dot{P}_{t-1}^e + \lambda_2(\dot{P}_{t-1} - \dot{P}_{t-2}^e) \qquad (3.22)$$

We can see that the second order component will only affect expectations when $\dot{P}_{t-2}^e$ is not equal to $\dot{P}_{t-1}$. Yet these two variables can still be equal when people take into account the rate of change in inflation when forming their expectations. This will happen, for example, when those expectations are correct.

An alternative interpretation of their conclusion that a more complex forecasting method seemed to be employed after 1967 may be that the rate of inflation was both more variable and, on average, much higher after that date. It might be that this reflected an underlying change in the inflation generating mechanism, for example, viewing inflation as an ARIMA (p, d, q) process with a change in either the parameters, p, d or q, or at least a perceived change. Alternatively it may be that with the higher inflation rates the costs of being in error had increased. As a result of these changes the optimal method of forecasting changed to a second order learning mechanism.

We therefore have two possible interpretations for the apparent change in forecasting after 1967. The first is that the ARIMA process changed, or was believed to have changed from an ARIMA $(p, 1, q)$ process, for example, to an ARIMA $(p, 2, q)$ process, and that as a result of this change individuals began forming their expectations about the rate of change of inflation, rather than inflation itself. In the terminology adopted by Fleming (1976) people had changed up a gear in their expectation formation mechanism. Alternatively we could view the process as having changed in such a way that the expected error variances of the various methods of expectation had changed. Because of this a more complex second order learning mechanism was now optimal.

This study by Carlson and Parkin also provides some evidence in favour of a mixed rational–adaptive hypothesis. This comes from the significance of the devaluation dummy, implying that this increased people's inflationary expectations. Thus, these equations furnish some support for the hypothesis that, although expectations seem to be formed in an adaptive manner, and not in a rational way based upon some model of the economy, external factors are sometimes taken into account. This implies that although the population as a whole is not in possesion of a complete economic model of the inflationary process, neither are they in complete ignorance of such a model. They are able to link certain events with changes in the inflation rate.

However these results rest upon the quality of the data Carlson and Parkin use, and this in turn rests upon the method they use to convert the qualitative responses from the survey into quantitative form. This method has been criticised by Foster and Gregory (1977) who particularly question whether the distribution of expectations across individuals is normal, as Carlson and Parkin assumed. They cite evidence by Carlson

(1975) who rejects the normality assumption for the Livingstone data, reporting distributions showing more positive skewness in periods when inflation was strong or accelerating, and more negative skewness when deflation was considered possible. If this evidence could be carried over to the Carlson–Parkin data then their series would be characterised by a systematic downward bias at cyclical peaks coupled with an upward bias in troughs. Secondly, as the overall trend of prices throughout the whole period was upwards, this will result in a downward bias throughout, particularly for the second half of that period. But because the average expected rate of inflation is made equal to the average rate over the whole period, this will result in underprediction from 1970 onwards, to be offset by overprediction prior to this.

There are also difficulties in applying the method when there is a zero response in any category, for example, nobody expecting prices to fall. Carlson and Parkin encountered several such periods, and Foster and Gregory argue that the method adopted to cope with these will result in an upward bias. These criticisms cast some doubt on the validity of the Carlson–Parkin data. The normality assumption in particular seems unlikely to be valid. This seems to be borne out by the data, for although the general trend in expectations seems to follow that of the actual inflation rate, there does seem to be a systematic downward bias from the beginning of 1971 onwards. In particular one notes that in the three years 1971–3 the expectations series exceeded the actual series in only four months.

But perhaps the chief problem with the data lies with the problems associated with periods when inflation and expectations of inflation are both high. Carlson and Parkin favour, as we have seen, the adaptive expectations hypothesis. In this case differences in expectations presumably arise due to differences in adjustment coefficients, perceptions and individual shopping baskets. But such differences cannot possibly result in anybody expecting prices to fall when prices themselves have not fallen for any length of time during the whole of the postwar period. Much the same comments apply if one asumes that expectations are formed either extrapolatively or rationally. If then we are to accept any of these hypotheses, we must also accept that the expectations of those who expect prices to fall are formed in a way not representative of the majority of the population. As such we can deduce little about the behaviour of the majority from these deviants.

This does not invalidate all of their conclusions. For example, it seems likely that if the exogenous impact of devaluation was great on the deviant, it probably also influenced the calculations of the majority. But considerable doubt is cast upon the parameters they estimate, and also the validity of using these data as a proxy for expectations in a wage equation.

A similar method for converting qualitative into quantitative data was developed by Knobl (1974). He essentially used the same method as Carlson and Parkin, although he explained it within a slightly different framework. It is therefore open to much the same criticisms as is theirs. The data are based upon the responses of German businessmen, for the period 1965–73, to the question of whether they expect the selling price to rise, fall or stay the same in the next three to four months, the survey seeming to have been carried out every quarter. Unlike Carlson and Parkin's data these do not represent the opinions of the general public about the future course of prices as a whole, which of course they have no direct influence upon. Instead they relate to the expectations of one specific section of the community, whose behaviour may or may not be representative of the remainder, about one specific good, or a limited number of goods, about which they have intimate knowledge and whose price they ultimately determine.

When he tested methods of expectation formation with this data he found that the adaptive expectations hypothesis did not give good results, but that regressions with lagged inflation rates as the only explanatory variables did. When in addition a demand pressure variable was included in the regression the results were

$$\dot{P}_t^e = 1.1146 + 0.2876\dot{P}_t + 0.3536(\dot{P}_t - \dot{P}_{t-1}) + 0.2589\mathrm{DP}_{t-1}$$
$$(4.83)(3.09)(2.43)(4.65)$$

$$\bar{R}^2 = 0.892 \tag{3.23}$$

$$\mathrm{DW} = 0.598$$

where the numbers in parentheses represent t statistics, and DP_{t-1} is a lagged measure of the pressure of demand. It should be noted that the Durbin–Watson statistic is far from satisfactory in this and his other equations. However, if we ignore this we may construe these results as providing further support for a rational–extrapolative hypothesis.

Yet another set of data has been derived by Paunio and Suvanto (1977), on a monthly basis, by looking at the difference between indexed and non-indexed bonds issued by the Finnish government. The index clause generally provided for 50 per cent compensation for rises in the consumer price index. Because the number of dealers in the bond market is small, consisting mainly of banks and private bankers, they felt that these expectations were representative of the well informed section of the business community and not of the public as a whole.

When price expectations are held with certainty a measure for expectations can be found by subtracting the rate of interest on the indexed linked bond from that on the other, and then adjusting for the proportion of index linkage, this being the straightforward Fisherian approach. However, when investors are not risk neutral and when expectations are not held with complete certainty, the calculations are not so simple. Paunio and Suvanto overcame these problems by assuming, as did Carlson and Parkin within a different context, that the expected rate of change in prices is equal to the actual rate of change in the long run. It should also be noted that in order to make these calculations they divided the period into two, 1963(1)–1968(3) and 1968(4)–1974(12), as around 1968 'there occurred several institutional changes which may have affected the formation of expectations'. The difficulties with this approach centre on the manner in which the uncertainty problem is circumvented. They assumed a linear risk aversion function, where risk is measured by the standard deviation of the expected value of the total return, and that this is constant during times of high and low inflation.

Having obtained these data they then tested a first order adaptive expectations mechanism. They also tested a second order mechanism, but this did not improve the results. These were

$$\dot{P}^e_t = 0.305\dot{P}_{t-1} + 0.720\dot{P}^e_{t-1}$$
$$(3.7) \qquad (9.1)$$

$$\bar{R}^2 = 0.777$$

$$DW = 1.61 \qquad\qquad (3.24)$$

and

$$\dot{P}^e_t = 0.120\dot{P}_{t-1} + 0.885\dot{P}^e_{t-1}$$
$$(2.3) \qquad (15.17)$$

$$\bar{R}^2 = 0.889$$

$$DW = 1.93 \qquad\qquad (3.25)$$

where (3.24) refers to the first period and (3.25) the second; t statistics are again in parentheses. They adjudged these results to be satisfactory, although one slightly puzzling aspect to them was that, uniquely, lagged inflation appeared to have been used in these regressions, although no comment was made upon this.

Less satisfactory was the simple extrapolative model of the form in

(3.1), with both the $\bar{R}^2$ and the Durbin–Watson statistic being on the low side. They also tested a regressive–extrapolative model, but again the results were not good. Finally they found that the devaluation of October 1967, by 31 per cent, had an impact effect which served to increase expectations by nearly 4 per cent.

More recently Jacobs and Jones (1980) have put forward a multi-level adaptive expectations model, where expectations are based upon a two-stage procedure. Individuals first compute their best estimate of the price level, $P_t^{e'}$, inflation rate, $\pi_t^{e'}$, and drift in the inflation rate, $d_t^{e'}$, which occurred for the period $t-1$ to t.

$$P_t^{e'} = P_t^e + \lambda_1 (P_t - P_t^e) \tag{3.26}$$

$$\pi_t^{e'} = \pi_t^e + \lambda_2 (P_t - P_t^e) \tag{3.27}$$

$$d_t^{e'} = d_t^e + \lambda_3 (P_t - P_t^e) \tag{3.28}$$

where expectations without a prime denote that these were held in $t-1$, while those with a prime are the revised estimates based on information available in period t. Individuals then use these to forecast for the interval t to $t+1$, for example,

$$P_{t+1}^e = P_t^{e'} + \pi_t^{e'} + d_t^{e'} \tag{3.29}$$

In the empirical work, which was based upon the Livingstone data for the USA, the drift factor was insignificant at the 95 per cent level of significance. Hence its role must be somewhat dubious in the above formulation. The real importance of their work lies in their recognition that the observed value of the price level in period t, P_t, might not correspond to individual's perceptions of the underlying trend, P_t^e, as was also the case with the Kalman filter. One slightly puzzling aspect to their work is that all three expectations adapt to the forecast error in the price level rather than the specific variable with which they are concerned.

Most of the studies we have looked at so far have tested versions of adaptive or extrapolative theories. However, Mullineaux (1980b), again using the Livingstone data, was concerned with testing some aspects of the rational expectations hypothesis. He concluded that, in addition to past inflation rates, lagged rates of money growth systematically affected the forecasts, but not measures of fiscal policy. Furthermore, he found that, using Cooley and Prescott's varying parameter regression technique, the influence of both money growth and of the most recently observed inflation rate appears to have increased over time. He therefore concluded that the Livingstone data are consistent with the rational expectations hypothesis, although his results are also consistent with a joint rational–extrapolative hypothesis.

This conclusion is in conflict with those reached by Feige and Pearce (1976). They cross-correlated innovations in inflation with innovations in monetary or fiscal variables and found to their surprise that the two were largely independent. The hypothesis of rationality has also been rejected by Pesando (1975), although he used the original Livingstone data, uncorrected by Carlson. His test of rationality was that the coefficients relating actual inflation to lagged inflation should be the same as those relating expected inflation to lagged inflation. This was found to be the case for expectations relating to period $t + 1$, but not for those relating to period $t + 2$. This Pesando describes as a weak test of rationality, since autoregressive forecasts will only be fully rational under very restrictive circumstances. But the fact that the data fail to pass even this test suggests to him that they would also fail to pass stronger versions of the hypothesis. The problem with this is that Pesando is not only rejecting the rational expectations hypothesis, but most extrapolative hypotheses as well. For he suggests that forecasts for inflation for the period $t + 1$ cannot simply be extrapolated to obtain forecasts for $t + 2$. Moreover he does not suggest what theory of expectation formation is consistent with his results, although it is possible that an extrapolative scheme with regressive elements might be appropriate. However, it should be borne in mind that the work was done with the original Livingstone data which is statistically defective, and the same conclusions might not be reached if the corrected data were used.

The results of these various studies are summarised in Table 3.2, and though at first glance there appears to be considerable differences between them, a deeper inspection reveals some consistency between the findings. First, several of the studies note a difference in expectation formation in times when inflation is high compared with times when it is low, when a simpler forecasting mechanism is employed. Secondly, several of the studies find a rational element in expectation formation which augments the basic extrapolative/adaptive mechanism. However, there seems no general consensus as to which of the models of expectation formation is the best one. This lack of agreement may be because of the inadequacies of the data, and this possibility should not be underestimated. However it may also reflect the fact that the expectations in the various studies are formed by different sets of people and relating to different subjects. Thus it should not really surprise us if American business and academic

Table 3.2   Summary of the various studies of expectation formation

Study	Frequency and revision period	'Optimal model'	Expectations held by
Turnovsky and Wachter	6 months	Rational model	Business and academic economists (USA)
Turnovsky pre-1964	6 months	Basically constant, with some correction for past trends	Business and academic economists (USA)
Turnovsky post-1964	6 months	Both adaptive and extrapolative work well	Business and academic economists (USA)
Jacobs and Jones	6 months	Modified form of adaptive expectations	Business and academic economists (USA)
Mullineaux	6 months	Rational expectations, with the rational element becoming more important over time	Business and academic economists (USA)
Carlson and Parkin 1961–7	1 month	Expectations basically autoregressive	General public (UK)
Carlson and Parkin 1967–73	1 month	A second order error learning mechanism, with the 1967 devaluation of the pound having a significant impact	General public (UK)
Knobl	3 months	Rational–extrapolative model	West German businessmen
Paunio and Suvanto	1 month	Rational–adaptive model	The well-informed section of the Finnish business community

economists seem to form some of their forecasts in accordance with economic theory. The relevant question is whether this can be generalised to other expectations held by other sections of the community. The increasing importance of monetary factors in expectation formation noted by Mullineaux, if valid, is probably a reflection of the growing acceptance of monetarist theories amongst economists. It is not, however, valid to go on to conclude that the population as a whole has also been as impressed and aware of these theories.

There are also other differences between the studies. One important one is the difference in the frequency with which the data become available. This ranges from every six months for the Livingstone data to every month for the Carlson and Parkin series. This is important as nearly all researchers have assumed a revision period equal to the frequency at which the data become available. Hence Carlson and Parkin assume expectations to be revised every month, whereas Turnovsky and Wachter have a minimum revision period of six months. Which, if any, of these is correct will depend upon how frequently actual expectations are revised. At the individual level it might be supposed that the shortest possible revision period will correspond to the frequency with which the individual comes into contact with the relevant stimulus. When, for example, the expectations concern the rate of inflation of the general price level, the stimulus occurs every time the individual buys a commodity or hears of a coming price rise. In actual fact the revision period may well be longer than this and may, like the actual method of expectation formation, be the outcome of an optimising process by the individual. Thus it may be that when the actual inflation rate is subject to severe fluctuations the revision period is much shorter than when it is relatively stable. Another major factor may be the use for which the expectations are to be put. If, for example, this is solely to judge the worth of money wage offers, then we might suppose the revision period to be related to the frequency with which wage contracts are negotiated. However, in the aggregate expectations are likely to be a much smoother function of time than for the individual, and it may be that the revision period then becomes so short as to be almost continuous.

The consequences of assuming a too long revision period will be to increase the error term in the equation, thus biasing the results against acceptance of the adaptive expectations hypothesis. One can imagine situations where expectations are revised weekly in an adaptive manner, but if a six-month revision period is used the explanatory power of the adaptive expectations hypothesis becomes quite poor. To some, though perhaps to a lesser extent, these comments also apply to other tests of expectation formation. It must be stressed therefore that what Turnovsky and Wachter are in fact testing is not simply the adaptive expectations hypothesis, but the adaptive expectations hypothesis with a six-month revision period. Bearing this in mind it is perhaps significant that the adaptive expectations hypothesis seems to work best in those studies that assume a relatively short revision period.

From all this we can see that the empirical work on expectations has been far from satisfactory. Basically this is because good, relevant data about expectations are simply not available. Either the data themselves are satisfactory, but the expectations are held by the wrong people about the wrong subject, or, alternatively, the characteristics of the expectations are relevant for economic theory but their quality is dubious. This is not to criticise the economists who have worked in this field. Information about expectation formation is vitally important in many areas of economics, and these economists have made valiant attempts to provide that information, and because of the importance of the subject, their work is also important. But it is also important to realise the limitations of their work, and the very serious qualifications that must be placed against their conclusions. Above all it is important to realise the need for good, relevant data about expectations, and the only satisfactory source of this is the government statistical service. It is highly desirable that they conduct a regular sample survey of the public to determine their expectations, not just about inflation, but also several other areas of ignorance which are proving serious stumbling blocks in economic research.

Incorporating Expectations into the Wage Equation

There have been three main approaches to the problem of incorporating expectations into the wage equation, using directly observed data, generating a series using some formula, or attempting to incorporate the expectation formation process into the specification of the basic model. To some extent the results of introducing expectations into the wage equation have been dealt with in the first chapter, and we are now more concerned with the general validity of these three methods.

The appropriateness of using directly observed data, as, for example, Parkin, Sumner and Ward (1976) and Riddel (1979) have done, with the Carlson–Parkin and Livingstone data, respectively, depends upon the accuracy of that data. In the previous sections serious question marks were raised on this point, and I feel that the validity of such work is questionable. The second method also depends upon the underlying validity of the model, and the parameters used to generate the series. In particular I have grave reservations about the use of one formula to generate expectations over a long period of time. For, as was emphasised earlier, it seems likely that different methods of expectation formation are employed at different times, with more complex methods being used when inflation is high or the inflation process is perceived to have changed.

The third method consists of including the expectation formation process within the general empirical structure of the model to be estimated, when, for example, expectations are formed according to a first order adaptive mechanism as in (3.3) and the wage equation is

$$\dot{W}_t = f(X_t) + \dot{P}_t^e + u_t \tag{3.30}$$

where X_t represents the explanatory variables, other than expectations, and u_t is an error term. Then lagging this one period and rearranging we get

$$\dot{P}_{t-1}^e = \dot{W}_{t-1} - f(X_{t-1}) - u_{t-1} \tag{3.31}$$

Combining this with (3.30) and (3.3) we get

$$\dot{W}_t = f(X_t) + \lambda \dot{P}_t - (1-\lambda)f(X_{t-1}) + (1-\lambda)\dot{W}_{t-1} + u_t - (1-\lambda)u_{t-1}$$

$$\tag{3.32}$$

We can estimate this, the only difficulties being that the equation, when estimated by ordinary least squares, tends to get lengthy and there is the problem of induced negative serial correlation as indicated by the composite error term in (3.32).

Rational expectations can, in theory, also be incorporated into the empirical specification of the model. In the case where they are based on lagged changes in the money supply this specification can be included in the structure of the model very easily. In the more general case, where the expectations are based on all the relevant information available at time t, then the estimation process becomes more difficult (see Wallis, 1980).

Both of these approaches have been open to the same criticism made previously, that in general they imply the same method of expectation formation regardless of the economic conditions. In addition, the latter approach suffers from all the criticisms we have made against the rational expectations hypothesis.

Thus economists attempting to proxy expectations are faced with a difficult choice, knowing that whatever they do it will not be entirely satisfactory. They can either use directly observed data which are often of dubious quality or alternatively they can incorporate, directly or indirectly, within the model some mechanistic form of expectation formation, which is insensitive to changing economic conditions and is in any case often of dubious validity in itself.

The Formation of Wage Inflation Expectations in the United Kingdom

The data we are going to use, which have been described fully elsewhere (Hudson, 1978), are derived from the *Financial Times* Survey of Business Opinion. This is carried out monthly for the *Financial Times* by the Taylor Nelson Group who collect the data by means of personal interviews with the chairmen, managing directors and other executive directors of public companies. The sample is based upon the 400 companies that constitute the *Financial Times* actuaries index. To provide a workable sampling framework the thirty industrial groupings of that index have been reduced to twelve major categories, the first two, for example, being electrical engineering and building materials. Each month three groups are surveyed, which means that the whole index is covered every four months, with non-electrical engineering, a particularly large and important group, being surveyed every two months. About a dozen interviews are obtained in each of the three groups, making an average of thirty to forty interviews a month.

The data for wage expectations come in the form of a frequency distribution. The figures are four-monthly moving totals, representing the expectations of all eleven industrial groupings. Those under the heading September–December are assumed to represent expectations in the middle of that period, that is, on November 1. In order to find the mean of this distribution we make the assumption that the proportion who did not answer had expectations distributed in similar proportions to those who did, and the percentage of answers falling in each interval was adjusted accordingly. Although the survey has been published continuously since it began, not all the data are suitable. This is because during the periods December 1969–October 1971 and February 1975–June 1975 more than 50 per cent of the replies fell in open-ended categories. Consequently the empirical work has been done by combining together all those observations that fell outside these two periods. This has one unfortunate consequence arising from the fact that we omit periods where expectations reached unprecedented heights. This being an omission on the basis of the dependent variable, may induce sample selection bias in the results.

The data are shown in Figure 3.1, along with actual inflation, which is

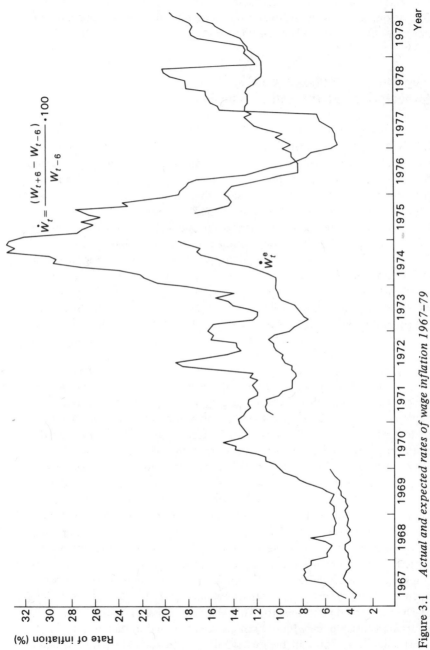

Figure 3.1   *Actual and expected rates of wage inflation 1967–79*
Sources: *Financial Times Survey of Business Opinion* and *Monthly Digest of Statistics*, various issues

the annual rate of inflation centred on the month immediately previous to the one in which the expectations are formed. Thus if expectations are held on November 1, the rate of wage inflation is centred on October. This is intended as a proxy for the underlying rate of inflation in October. In defining the independent variable in this way we are making a fundamental departure from previous studies, which typically assumed that the period people consider when revising their expectations is the same length as that for which they are held. For example, if expectations are formed for the coming twelve months, then it is usually the previous twelve months which are taken as the relevant stimuli. Instead of this we shall assume that the relevant period to consider when revising expectations is equal to the frequency with which expectations are revised. Thus if expectations are revised at monthly intervals, as we are assuming here, then people will consider the events of the previous month when adapting their expectations from those which were held in the previous month. The alternative view implies that people change or adapt their expectations every month on the basis of what has happened in the previous twelve months. Yet surely the spirit of the adaptive expectations hypothesis implies that people will only adapt their expectations to take account of information that was not previously available.

It was decided to proxy the underlying rate of inflation in a given month in this way because of the high noise-to-signal ratio in the monthly wage inflation series. This varies not only with the underlying rate of inflation, which constitutes the signal element, but also with the number of wage settlements, which is a major constituent of the noise component. A large number of settlements, or a few very important ones, will cause the wage index to rise by an unusually large amount, and vice versa. The individual can easily filter out the signal from the noise element. He has extra information relating to the size of settlements and any special circumstances surrounding them, which will enable him to readily form a fairly accurate view of the underlying rate of wage inflation. Such information is not easily discernible in government statistics, and we have been forced to use the annual rate of wage inflation centred on that month as a proxy for the underlying trend, in a similar manner as, for example, Lipsey (1960).

This is not a perfect proxy, but I feel that it is the best available in current circumstances. However, its use brings us further problems, which are mainly the result of the effects of the social contract, that is, the Labour government's incomes policy which began in August 1975. This had the effect of altering the normal pattern of wage settlements, having particularly pronounced effects once the incomes policy began to break down from the end of July 1977 onwards. This is a possible reason for the violent fluctuations in this measure of inflation which occurred from about this time. I feel that this reduces the usefulness of this measure of inflation and have consequently restricted the empirical work to end in 1976.

From Figure 3.1 it can be seen that, prior to 1976, expectations were always below the underlying rate of inflation. One possible explanation for this might be that, within the context of the adaptive expectations hypothesis, an extremely small first order adjustment coefficient, is coupled with a larger second order coefficient, which is operative in certain periods only, but only if it were combined with a rational element where, for example, the introduction of incomes policies had an impact effect upon expectations. However, there is an alternative explanation which must also be considered — that people do not always correctly perceive the rate of inflation. The problem of perception has been largely ignored within the literature, apart from Carlson and Parkin's reference to a difference limen. But upon consideration it becomes clear that the correct specification of the simple adaptive expectations hypothesis, for example, should be conceived in terms of the perceived rate of inflation rather than the actual rate of inflation. It is therefore an implicit assumption in most of the empirical work that the inflation rate is fully perceived. However, with no data on perceptions we can go no further with this line of thought at this time.

Table 3.3   *Incomes policies introduced in the sample period*

Details	Date introduced
3½% ceiling on pay increases, except those associated with productivity	20 March 1968
CBI (employers' association) asks industry to avoid price increases over following twelve months, or to limit them to 5% in unavoidable cases	15 July 1971
90-day statutory freeze	6 November 1972
Freeze extended by 60 days	17 January 1973
Phase II, pay increases restricted to £1 + 4% of average wage bill	1 April 1973
Phase III, pay increases restricted to £2.25 or 7% of average wage bill plus threshold agreements (a form of index linking)	1 November 1973
Government adopted £6 a week policy	9 July 1975
Chancellor suggests a pay limit of 3%, finally agrees to one of 4½% with the unions	6 April 1976

Several hypotheses of expectation formation were tested, including general extrapolative and rational expectations. But the ones which tended to work best were variants of the adaptive expectations hypothesis. It was also found that the introduction of incomes policies often tended to have a downward impact effect upon expectations. These are listed in Table 3.3. Partly due to the difficulties of allowing for the effects of incomes policies within a regression equation these periods were also omitted in estimating the regressions which are reported below. Of the several forms of adaptive expectations that were tested, those where expectations were based on two different mechanisms, with the more complex one being employed in certain periods only, gave the best results. The theoretical basis for such a mechanism was given earlier. A change to a more complex mechanism will occur when the structure of the inflationary process changes so that this complex mechanism becomes optimal in the sense defined by Feige and Pearce. One possibility is that a second order mechanism, for example, becomes relevant when the underlying parameters of the actual inflation rate series appear to have changed, as a result of which a first order mechanism no longer produces optimal forecasts, as the expected mean square error of the first order mechanism has increased. If therefore we could isolate those periods when such a change occurred we could restrict the second order variables to be operative in those periods alone. The criterion adopted for identifying such periods was that the actual rate of inflation had been increasing (or decreasing) for four or more successive months by more than 0.1 percentage points. If in succeeding months the rate of inflation fell and then rose (or vice versa) the second order element would not be operative in the first month, but would be so in the second.

There are two possible justifications for assuming that such periods are ones of perceived structural change. First, in such periods people's perceptions of the underlying time series might change from ARIMA $(p, 1, q)$ to ARIMA $(p, 2, q)$. In other words, a person might, in the changed situation, be forming expectations not just about the rate of inflation but also about its rate of change, although a second order error learning mechanism is not perhaps the best way of doing this. Secondly, if the proposed structural change takes the form of a change in the parameters of an ARIMA $(p, 1, q)$ process, then a more complex mechanism may become optimal during the transition period, as individuals learn the parameters of the new structure. A continual increase, or decrease, in the inflation rate will then be the signal for structural change.

The results of including this 'occasional second order mechanism' within the basic adaptive expectations model were as follows:

$$\dot{W}_t^e = 0.98\dot{W}_t^e + 0.02\dot{W}_t + 0.53\dot{W}_{t-1}^{e'} - 0.62\dot{W}_{t-2}^{e'} + 0.08\dot{W}_t' - 0.02\dot{W}_{t-1}'$$
$$\quad\;\; (26.20)\quad (0.70)\;\; (3.22)\qquad (4.13)\qquad (1.15)\quad (0.26)$$

$$R^2 = 0.99$$

$$DW = 1.60 \tag{3.33}$$

where the numbers in parentheses represent t statistics, and a prime denotes that that variable was operative only during periods of perceived structural change as defined above. Both the R^2 and the Durbin–Watson statistic are relatively satisfactory. However, this result provides little support for the amended second order error learning hypothesis. None of the coefficients on lagged inflation is significant at the 10 per cent level of significance. As a consequence the equation was re-estimated, but omitting $\dot{W}_t'$ and $\dot{W}_{t-1}'$. The results were:

$$\dot{W}_t^e = 0.93\dot{W}_{t-1}^e + 0.05\dot{W}_t + 0.70\dot{W}_{t-1}^{e'} - 0.69\dot{W}_{t-2}^{e'}$$
$$\quad\;\; (34.29)\qquad (2.82)\quad (5.11)\qquad (5.02)$$

$$R^2 = 0.99$$

$$DW = 1.85 \tag{3.34}$$

Again both the Durbin–Watson statistic and the explanatory power of the equation are satisfactory, although it should be noted that as a lagged dependent variable is present the Durbin–Watson statistic will be biased towards 2. The economic interpretation of this regression is that in normal times expectations are formed according to a simple first order mechanism. But in periods of perceived structural change, in addition to this basic mechanism the change in expectations lagged one period, that is $\dot{W}_{t-1}^e - \dot{W}_{t-2}^e$ is an important element in expectation formation. Such a mechanism combines part of the appeal of both the adaptive and rational expectations hypotheses. It can be seen that it possesses the simplicity of adaptive expectations, but without the undesirable property that during an upswing or downswing expectations continually lag behind actual inflation, giving rise to systematic and very predictable forecasting errors.

It should be noted that the sum of the two first order coefficients is less than 1. The implication of this is that in equilibrium, that is, when both the inflation rate and actual expectations remain unchanged, expectations will not equal the rate of inflation. For example, if the rate of inflation is 7 per cent, then in equilibrium expectations will equal 5 per cent. One interpretation of this might be that inflation is not being fully perceived.

Chapter 4

Inflation in the United Kingdom and the United States

Inflation in the United Kingdom

We now come to examine how well our theory can explain the course of inflation in the UK and the USA, beginning with the UK. Figure 4.1 shows the course of wage inflation, price inflation and the unemployment rate over the period 1950–80. The first part of this period, until 1970, may perhaps be seen as one in which inflation by itself was regarded as a major problem only in as much as it affected the balance of payments. It has been characterised as a period of stop–go policies, in which the government would first deflate and then reflate the economy as its attention was concentrated on first the balance of payments and then the level of unemployment. It begins in the immediate postwar period, with both wages and prices increasing rapidly. As a response to this the then Labour government introduced what was to be one of the most successful attempts at an incomes policy. This had the immediate effect of reducing the inflation rate despite continuing supply side shortages, in particular labour. However, such controls were abandoned with the election of a Conservative government, and partly because of this and partly because of the Korean War wages and prices once more began increasing rapidly. From then until 1964 deflation and reflation were to succeed each other in fairly rapid succession. On need the government was always able to increase or decrease the level of unemployment, using the traditional means of fiscal and monetary policy, that is, tax rates, government expenditure and interest rates, an ability which those who argue for government impotency in this area would do well to consider.

Take, for example, the period 1957–60, the beginning of which was marked by a crisis in July and August of 1957, which saw a large scale withdrawal of funds from London. In retrospect this seems mainly to have been caused by external factors, as the current account was at this time in comfortable surplus. In August the French franc was effectively devalued and this fed rumours of other possible currency realignments, which for the pound meant devaluation. None the less attention was focused on

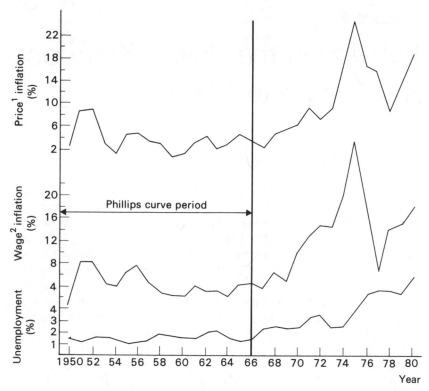

Figure 4.1   *Inflation and unemployment in the UK.*
Source: *Economic Trends Annual Abstract*, 1981
Notes: 1. Retail price index
        2. Basic weekly wages, all industries, all workers

domestic causes, which it was felt were making the UK uncompetitive. One factor which disturbed many was the emergence of an annual wage round following the inflation associated with the Korean War. Partly in response to this feeling the then Chancellor of the Exchequer set up, in 1957, the Council on Prices, Productivity, and Incomes, in an embryonic attempt to influence wages and prices independently of the level of demand. This was, however, accompanied by a set of deflationary measures in September of that year. These, or at least the rhetoric which surrounded them, have a familiar ring. The aim was to control certain monetary aggregates, particularly government expenditure and bank advances. This it was argued would lead to unemployment only if the unions pursued excessive wage claims. Partly because of these measures unemployment increased and inflation fell throughout 1957 and into 1958, although a fall in world commodity prices was also a factor in the latter. With this, and with the restoration of relative calm on the international money markets, attention shifted once more to expansionist policies. During 1958 various expansionary steps were taken, which were supplemented by considerable tax reductions in the 1959 Budget. The effects of these were again to reduce unemployment and increase inflation, and the period ends with the government facing renewed worries about the balance of payments.

In several respects 1964 marks a watershed in government policy. First, stop–go policies were largely abandoned, and since then the emphasis has been much more on deflationary policies, with the level of unemployment showing an almost constant increase. Secondly, governments have been much readier to contemplate direct controls on wages and prices. In the earlier period incomes policies were resorted to only once, in 1961. Since then they have alternated with pure deflationary policies, as each in turn fails to achieve stability in the price level. The first such attempt was in July 1966 when the recently elected Labour government introduced a total freeze on wages, followed by a period of 'severe restraint'. These actions were taken because of continuing problems on the foreign exchange markets, despite the fact that the rate of increase in wages was relatively modest. None the less these policies had some success in moderating the rate of inflation still further. However, when the period of severe restraint ended in July 1967 these effects diminished. Both wage and price inflation accelerated, despite the fact that unemployment was also high and increasing. Further attempts at direct controls were to follow, again coupled with a battery of deflationary measures. But inflation seemed to be gaining a resilience against such effects and showed few signs of slowing down.

In 1970 an incoming Conservative government, spurning the use of direct controls, turned the deflationary screw still further, mainly in the form of public expenditure cuts which increased the level of unemployment still further. Yet despite this, the earlier indication that inflation had broken free from the constraints of the Phillips curve were confirmed. Inflation, to everyone's surprise, actually increased and increased at an alarmingly rapid rate, pushing the annual rate of wage increases up to nearly 14 per cent, which represented a postwar record, despite the fact that unemployment was also at a postwar record. By 1971 the government began edging towards a prices and incomes policy, a process that was made harder as earlier deflationary policies had been accompanied by attempts at 'trade union reform'. These reflected the general belief, which is still prevalent, that trade unions are a major obstacle to the achievement of a stable price level. But these reforms so antagonised the trade union movement that any possibility of a voluntary agreement over incomes was effectively ruled out. As a consequence a series of statutory policies followed in quick succession, as can be seen from Table 3.3. These had the effect of stabilising the rate of wage and price inflation, despite the fact that reflationary policies were momentarily causing unemployment to fall. The government, partially freed from balance of payments problems by the decision to float the pound in June 1972 and the promise of North Sea oil, hoped that this might secure the co-operation of the unions in future incomes policies. But such hopes were doomed to failure and in two damaging strikes the miners effectively defeated the government's policies. The second of these strikes began with an overtime ban from 12 November 1973. The government imposed a three-day working week from 1 January 1974 in an attempt to conserve fuel stocks. The dispute escalated into a full strike on 10 February, and the government responded by calling a general election which they subsequently lost.

The incoming Labour government, eschewing any attempt at a statutory incomes policy, attempted to move towards a voluntary agreement with the unions. Such attempts at first produced no real results, and both wage and price inflation accelerated rapidly to levels which began to draw comparisons with Latin American style inflations. These problems were further exacerbated by the first round of oil price increases at the end of 1973. These alone had a large deflationary effect on the British economy, and since then unemployment has been continually increasing. At the same time the crisis perhaps had the effect of persuading union leaders of the need for an incomes policy. In the event on 1 August an agreement became effective which limited wage increases to £6 a week, with further restrictions on prices. This was followed by additional measures in the following year. The effects were immediate and dramatic, and the social contract, as this agreement was called, must be viewed as one of the most successful of all attemps at controlling incomes, at least in the short run. But this success proved impossible to sustain, and the incomes policy effectively collapsed, if somewhat slowly, in the following year. The result was once more an acceleration in wage inflation with prices beginning to follow suit.

This was the situation facing the incoming Conservative government in May 1979, and they reacted in the traditional manner, by controlling government expenditure and the money supply, which effectively meant high interest rates. The result has been that unemployment has increased both at a speed and to a level which are totally without precedent in the postwar period. At first, price inflation accelerated upwards once more, partially as a result of a shift to indirect taxation, the effects of high interest rates on mortgage repayments, another round of world oil price increases, and increases in wage costs. But this increase has since moderated as these effects have to some extent dropped out of the calculations and firms are forced to accept lower profit margins in an attempt to clear stocks. Wage inflation also reacted perversely at first, but the most recent indications are that for the first time in more than a decade, this too seems to be moderating in response to excess supply. The question that now arises is whether this moderation will continue once the recession has ended.

There are several points of interest which arise from the discussion in this section. First, although the two series are largely coincident, it does seem that there is a slight tendency for wage inflation to lead price inflation. For example, the peak in the wage inflation series in 1961 is followed one year later by a peak in the price inflation series. This is consistent with the argument advanced earlier that inflation is essentially – ignoring commodity price shocks – a labour market phenomenon. Excess demand first affects wages, and then mainly through this mechanism prices, rather than the other way round, as the monetarists would argue. Secondly, the government has repeatedly been able to influence the level of unemployment in a totally predictable way. There seems no support whatsoever for the concept of impotency in this area. Thirdly, we may note that it is perhaps only in the 1970s that inflation has been regarded as a major problem in its own right, rather than as simply an important factor in Britain's balance of payments problems. Finally it seems clear that the period can be divided into at least two fairly distinct sub-periods. In the first, which ended some time between 1966 and 1970, the Phillips curve mechanism worked well. As can be seen from Figure 4.1, each trough in the unemployment series was closely associated with a peak in the inflation series, particularly wage inflation. Similarly peaks in the unemployment series were accompanied by troughs in the inflation series. The relationship was systematic, predictable and well defined. However, the period since then seems to be one in which the relationship has almost completely broken down, with both inflation and unemployment being on a general upward trend, and not even the addition of expectations can rescue it. Only in the most recent months has there been some indication that inflation is once more responding to the promptings of unemployment.

A key test of the theory set out in Chapter 2 is whether it can explain both why the Phillips curve broke down when it did and why it recently seems to have been reborn. This is something to which we now turn to examine.

Explaining Inflation in the United Kingdom

In what we might call normal periods, that is, when the competitive wage exceeds the target wage, again defining these as averages across all employers and trade union leaders, there will be some strikes over wages. First, some industries will be in decline, and employers in those industries may have problems in negotiating with the unions. Similarly, some industries may have been experiencing periods of very high prosperity, which would lead workers to have higher than average expectations of income growth. When this prosperity declines to a more normal level, the employer will be unwilling to meet those expectations. We might also expect the number of strikes to vary with the business cycle due either to similar variations in the competitive wage or to union strategy.

However, when the competitive wage is less than the target wage in the average industry, rather than in the exceptional or isolated one, then wage bargaining will take on a much more genuine character. A strike will not always ensue for, as I argued earlier, in deciding whether and by how much to compromise, both union leaders and employers will have regard to the likely costs and benefits of a strike, both of which may vary with economic conditions. But we would expect that, other things being equal, the greater the gap between the average wage unions are demanding and that which employers wish to pay, then the greater is the likelihood of a strike. Thus when strikes are above some critical value, we can identify that period as one in which the target wage is greater than the competitive wage. In addition, the more strikes there are above this critical value, then the greater is the probable gap between the two sides. This measure will not be an exhaustive one, as it will not identify those periods where, for tactical reasons, the union leader decides not to pursue a strike at that time. Nor will it capture those periods in which the employer decides to accede to the union's demands rather than risk a strike, or some intermediate position between these two is reached.

Figure 4.2 shows the number of disputes over wages commencing in the relevant quarter, as published in the *Department of Employment Gazette*. These were published monthly, but do not represent all such strikes as some were reported after publication, and the amended figures were not published. Fortunately this does not seem too serious for our purposes as it seems unlikely to impart any bias to the analysis. The figures themselves represent the combination of two sets of strike categories, those relating to demands over wage advances, and those relating to other wage questions. Over the period as a whole there has been a shift in the relative importance of these two components, with strikes over wage advances becoming relatively more important. However, this may simply reflect the slight increase in the frequency with which wage rates are revised (see Elliot, 1976), the argument being that if wages are revised relatively infrequently, pressure for wage increases from workers will have to find outlets other than the obvious one of upward revision of the wage rate.

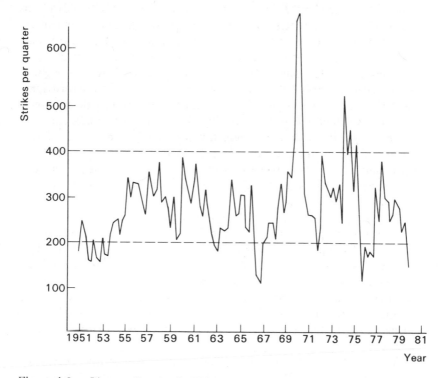

Figure 4.2   *Wage strikes in the UK*
Source: *Department of Employment Gazette*, various issues

These two categories of strikes combined showed no marked and sustained trend over the period as a whole. Instead what seems to have happened is some increase in the number of strikes in the early postwar years, reaching some form of plateau in 1955–6, from which the only deviations have been temporary. These deviations appear to have been of two kinds – steep troughs, as in 1963, and very sharp peaks as in 1969–70. It seems possible that we might identify some of the troughs with incomes policies, for such policies, although they do nothing to meet the workers' aspiration wages, reduce the immediate relevance of conflict between employer and employee. As for the relatively low level of strike activity in the early 1950s, this might be linked with the relative prosperity of that period, when few industries were in decline.

With regard to the peaks, two periods clearly stand out, 1969(4)–1970(3), and 1974(2)–1975(2). There were more than 400 wage strikes in seven out of these nine quarters, but not one in the remainder of the period. According to the theory previously developed this should indicate that in these nine quarters wages were being determined by a genuine bargaining process between employers and union leaders, with the target wage exceeding the competitive wage. Of course excessive strike activity is not the sole criterion for identifying such periods, in as much as there might be others where in general the bargaining process leads to an eventual agreement without a strike. However, it is at least suggestive that the nine quarters we have identified all occur in the 1970s when the Phillips curve had broken down. It is even more suggestive that the first four of these quarters occur exactly at the time that this break first became obvious. Thus it is perhaps not unreasonable to conclude that prior to this, when wage strikes never once rose above 400 per quarter, the competitive wage exceeded the target wage.

This, then, is my answer to the question posed earlier – the reason the Phillips curve broke down in 1970 was that in that year, apparently for the first time in the post Second World War era, the target wage exceeded the competitive wage. Prior to this the wages employers wanted to pay exceeded that which union leaders felt they needed to negotiate. Wages and wage inflation were therefore determined by the determinants of the competitive wage – the Phillips curve mechanism. In 1970 all that changed; the Phillips curve broke down and there was a large increase in wage strikes.

Since 1970 it would also appear likely that the competitive wage would have failed to exceed the target wage because of the very high levels of unemployment, mirroring slack labour market conditions, which, apart from a brief two-year period between 1972 and 1973, were typical of these years. If this is so one can only speculate as to why wage strikes were not excessive throughout this entire period. One important possibility is that after the wage explosion and rash of strikes in 1970 employers revised their estimates of the union's abilities to endure a strike, thus also revising upwards their estimates of the probable cost and duration of a strike. This would then cause them to be more likely to agree to a union's pre-strike demands. The second period of excessive strike activity coincides with the first round of oil price increases in 1973–4. These would almost certainly have fed through into price inflation expectations, thus raising the target wage. At the same time rapidly rising unemployment and deteriorating product market conditions would have been reducing the competitive wage. Thus the gap between the two sides would have increased, thereby increasing the gains for the employer from a refusal to satisfy the union's pre-strike position, and incurring a strike. Another point to bear in mind when examining the 1970s is that this period saw several incomes policies in operation. Some of these at least, particularly the Labour government's social contract, had a sizeable and direct effect on the bargaining process, and can probably explain some of the deep troughs in strike activity which we can see in Figure 4.2.

Thus, according to the above arguments, throughout most of the 1970s the Phillips curve mechanism would not have been a valid one with which to explain wage inflation. This I believe is the reason why empirical work done on the UK Phillips curve seems to indicate that after 1970 it no longer existed. In effect I am arguing that we have a switching regimes situation, with the Phillips curve operative in only part of this period. Attempting to estimate a Phillips curve for the whole of the period, or indeed for the whole of the post Second World War period, will therefore give invalid results.

A key element in the above argument is that suddenly, in 1969–70, the competitive wage no longer exceeded the target wage. The reason for this can be found by examining Figure 4.3. Until 1963 real net earnings deviated only temporarily from a fairly well defined upward trend. After that date they fell significantly below their trend level for several successive years. This, we suggest, was due to several factors: rapidly worsening labour market conditions which would have reduced the competitive wage, a series of tax increases which reduced the value of that wage to the worker, and a series of incomes policies which prevented unions from negotiating wages equal to their targets. Once attempts at formal controls on incomes were abandoned in the latter half of 1969 wage inflation increased sharply as unions tried, with considerable success, to achieve those targets.

The key to all this lies in changes in the labour market. Until the mid-1960s this was characterised by relatively low unemployment from which deviations were only minor and temporary. This coupled with a rate of productivity growth which, by historical standards, was extremely high meant that both wages and living standards increased rapidly. Inflation during this period was then largely caused by excess demand factors. In the mid-1960s this began to change, with unemployment rising to much higher levels. As a consequence of this the wages employers wanted to pay would have been unlikely to satisfy workers' aspirations. This might well have resulted in the breakdown of the Phillips curve even earlier than

1969–70, but for successive incomes policies. When these were abandoned there was still considerable slack in the labour market, and implicit contract considerations were probably dominant in determining the wages employers wanted to pay. None the less these would have been unlikely to satisfy workers' aspirations in full and an increase in strike activity and union membership was the result. The irrelevance of search considerations at this time also meant the demise, temporarily at least, of the Phillips curve.

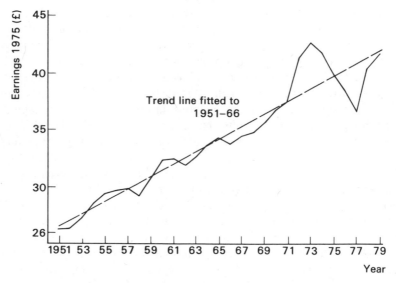

Figure 4.3   *Real net earnings in the UK for single full time adult male manual worker*
Source: *Department of Health and Social Security*

The reason why high unemployment had never before been associated with high inflation is that the rapid growth in real incomes in the first part of the period was without precedent. It is this phenomenon upon which expectations of, and aspirations for, rising real incomes are based. Prior to this there was no such base and therefore no such expectations. Probably the most that workers in, for example, the 1930s would have aspired to would have been to keep real incomes constant.

Turning now to the most recent period it does appear that the extremely high levels of unemployment in 1980 do seem to have had some success in reducing wage inflation. Within the context of our analysis this might be so for several reasons. First, it may be that the shock of this level of unemployment has had a direct effect on the permanent income calculations, such that previous trends will no longer be the sole factor in those calculations. In this case the government's policies will have been successful in reducing inflation, even in the long run. But it may also be that workers and their representatives have not abandoned their hopes of raising 'living standards, merely postponed their fulfilment, the reason being that, with so many firms near to closure and so many already unemployed, they may believe that this is not an opportune moment to press those claims. This is perhaps even more likely to be so because real net earnings in 1980 were probably not too far short of their permanent income levels, due to depressed prices and previous large wage increases. This would then also explain why there were also so few strikes. However, in this case when the economy moves out of the recession wage inflation may well accelerate once more.

Institutional Comparisons: the USA with the UK

There are several factors which distinguish the labour market in the USA from that in the UK. First, and most obviously, the proportion of the labour force which is unionised is much smaller than in the UK. This has also been declining in recent years and is now just over 20 per cent of the labour force compared with 50 per cent in the UK. This factor alone virtually rules out any theory of inflation that is based on trade unions and the bargaining process. Secondly, long-term contracts are common in the unionised sector in the USA. These contracts typically take the form of a first year increase, followed by deferred increases in the second and third years of the contract. Thus in 1980 80 per cent of workers in major bargaining units were under three-year contracts.

In addition to these planned increases, many long-term contracts contain provision for wages to increase in line with increases in the cost of living. Such escalator clauses first gained prominence in 1948, when General Motors and the United Auto Workers negotiated a two-year contract calling for quarterly wage adjustments to offset price increases. Since then escalator provisions have been adopted in a number of industries, their popularity tending to vary directly with the rate of inflation. As might be expected the 1970s saw a particularly rapid expansion of such agreements. Thus by January 1980 approximately 5.5 million workers under major collective bargaining agreements were covered by escalators, compared with only 3 million in 1970. Such cost of living adjustment (COLA) provisions tend to be concentrated in certain industries, more, for example, in manufacturing than in non-manufacturing. They are also more common in larger bargaining units than in smaller units. For example, in 1978 the average major bargaining unit covered about 4,600 employees, whereas those with COLA provisions covered about 4,800. Also, not surprisingly, such agreements are more common the longer the contract period.

In the original 1948 contract the escalator provision yielded pay adjustments that were approximately proportional to price changes. This also appears to have been the case in 1959 when Garberino (1962) reported that most of the COLA provisions fully compensated for price changes. This no longer seems to be the case today. In the ten-year period 1968–77, the average annual escalator increase, for workers in major bargaining units, ranged from 1.6 per cent in 1969 to 5.8 per cent in 1974. In no year did the increase match the rise in prices. The closest correspondence was in 1971 when escalator increases amounted to 91 per cent of price changes; the lowest was 26 per cent in 1969.

There are of course many other differences between the two economies. We have already mentioned the greater difficulties US administrations have had in managing the economy than their counterparts in London, largely due to differences in the relationship between the executive and legislative branches of government. However, the two differences we have highlighted have important implications for any analysis of inflation in the USA.

The first means that the analysis we made of the UK cannot simply be extended to the USA. The second makes any empirical work much more difficult for two reasons. First, wage increases in the third year of a three-year contract will probably be related more closely to conditions three years ago than present ones. Thus aggregate wage increases will be a much more complex function of labour market conditions than in the UK. This will also disturb the nature of the serial correlation, as will the variations in coverage of COLA contracts, thus making it more difficult to estimate any regression.

Inflation in the United States

Figure 4.4 shows the course taken by inflation in the postwar years, for both wages and prices. Both types of inflation follow the same general trend, although there are differences in individual years. The period begins in 1948 with both prices and wages rising at very rapid rates. This was to a large extent a result of the postwar boom and price inflation at least fell to a more acceptable level in 1949. The next major surge came in 1951 when again both price inflation and wage inflation were at very high rates. The

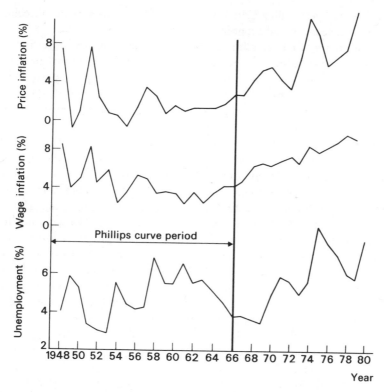

Figure 4.4   *Inflation and unemployment in the US*
Sources: *Economic Report of the President and Survey of Current Business*, various issues
Notes: 1. Consumer price index
2. Gross hourly average earnings
3. figures for 1980 are for May, they will therefore only approximately equal the actual figures for that year

level of unemployment at this time, as can also be seen from Figure 4.4, was 3.3 per cent which, although not excessively low, was a large decrease on the previous year's level. Thus this surge in inflation can be adequately explained by excess demand factors. Following this, controls were introduced for the Korean War period and both price and wage inflation moderated. From then until 1961 unemployment gradually rose and wage inflation fell. This was partly due to the restrictionist policies of the Eisenhower administration. The stability in the price level which followed was felt by many to have been bought at too high a price in terms of unused resources. It was also felt that, whether due to government policies or not, the USA was falling behind the rest of the world in terms of technological advancement and economic growth.

Thus in the 1960 election campaign Kennedy spoke of getting the country moving again. The incoming administration set an interim target for unemployment of 4 per cent. In the event recovery was slow, and in response Kennedy proposed to cut taxes in the beginning of 1963, but this, due to congressional opposition, was not enacted until early 1964. At the time of this tax cut unemployment was still at 5.5 per cent. Following it unemployment fell to the 4 per cent target by the following year. In the face of this, wage inflation began to accelerate again, although only moderately at first. Unemployment continued to fall until 1969, while inflation also continued to increase, and with it concern once more shifted away from unemployment to the stability of the price level. Thus in August 1967 the President proposed a 10 per cent surcharge on income tax to begin in October for individuals and retrospectively in July for corporations. However, Congress failed to pass this until mid-1968. This, despite reducing the budget deficit, failed to have much impact on inflation and unemployment, somewhat to the surprise of most observers at the time, and the incoming Nixon administration pledged itself to even tighter fiscal and monetary policies. They tightened up on federal expenditures and produced a budget surplus of some $9.5 billion in the first quarter of 1969, but still the economy continued to grow. However, by early 1970 business confidence began to decline and the effects on unemployment began to show. But there was no similar effect on inflation. For the first time in the postwar era, and quite possibly for the first time ever, a fall into a recession failed to curb the rate of wage inflation. Thus, slightly later than in the UK, the excess demand mechanism of the Phillips curve failed to work. It is true that by 1971 the rate of price inflation was beginning to subside, but the rate of wage inflation was greater than at any time since the Korean War, and showed no signs of slacking.

Faced with this situation the possibility of wage and price controls began to be discussed, and in August 1971 a programme was suddenly announced. It had three main parts. First, it attempted to restore the USA's competitive position vis-à-vis other countries, which had been steadily eroded by inflation. Secondly, it reduced selected taxes to stimulate recovery and hence reduce unemployment. Finally, it froze wages and prices for a period of ninety days, followed by a period of controlled increases for an indefinite time. The main purpose of these controls, according to the 1972 Annual Report of the Council of Economic Advisors, was to reduce expectations of inflation more quickly than would otherwise have been the case. Phase II of this policy was to be monitored by a price commission of seven members and a pay board of fifteen members. This latter body was divided equally between business, labour and the public interest. The guidelines were laid down at 2.5 per cent per year for price increases and 5.5 per cent for wages, with an allowance of up to 1.5 per cent for catching up. Under Phase II price inflation fell rapidly, although there has of course been controversy as to whether this was the result of controls or not. There was less discernible effect on wages, although first year changes in union contracts at 6.3 per cent in 1972 were almost half the rate of the preceding year.

Phase II was followed by Phase III when the administration relaxed the mandatory elements of the policy, substituting guidelines for most of the economy. The Cost of Living Council replaced the Price Commission and the Pay Board with authority to see that the guidelines were followed. There followed a period when wage inflation continued to moderate, with union wage increases falling still further. But price inflation accelerated once more, possibly due to firms attempting to restore profit margins cut in Phase II. This forced the administration into a new wage and price freeze in July 1973, which was followed by a Phase IV programme similar to Phase II. This failed to moderate the acceleration in wages and prices and this particular experiment in controls came to an end on 30 April 1974.

By then a new factor had emerged, the worldwide rise in commodity prices which reached a climax with the quadrupling of oil prices by OPEC late in 1973. The effect of this was immediate and dramatic. Price inflation rose to 11 per cent, nearly double what it had been in 1973. Unemployment also rose from 4.9 per cent in 1973 to 5.6 per cent in 1974 to 8.5 percent in 1975, this latter figure representing a postwar record. Wage inflation also increased, but by a lesser amount than price inflation. This sluggishness in wages was partly due to the prevalence of long-term contracts. In union contracts that were negotiated in 1974 the average first year change in wages was 9 per cent, as compared with 5.5 per cent in the previous year. It was also due to conditions in the non-unionised sectors, where wages did not increase by as much as in the unionised sectors.

The increase in unemployment occurred because with the increase in prices, real disposable income fell sharply. This led to a reduction in consumers' expenditure which affected business confidence and thus investment. All this, added to similar experiences in other countries which thus hit exports, spelt the beginning of a major recession. The steep decline in economic activity reached a climax in the first quarter of 1975. The administration responded with tax cuts and output recovered quickly with real GNP rising at an annual rate of 8.5 per cent in the second half of that year. However, excess capacity remained large and as can be seen unemployment began falling only very slowly, and by 1979 was still 5.8 per cent. The rate of price inflation also subsided slightly after the initial impact of the oil price rise had been absorbed. Wage inflation on the other hand continued to increase, and at 8.6 per cent in 1978 was higher than at any other time in the previous thirty years.

Finally in 1979–80 we come to the last dramatic surge in price inflation. In 1979 prices rose by 11.5 per cent. In 1980 they appear to be accelerating still further, with the consumer price index being 13.5 per cent above the average level in the previous year. The reason for this latest surge is not hard to find. Once more the rising cost of energy seems to be the reason, with the relevant component of the CPI almost doubling since 1978, following further OPEC price rises. Also important has been the increased cost of home ownership, which has risen by almost 40 per cent in the last two years, largely as a result of high interest rates. As in 1974 this sudden increase in the price level is having a significant effect on unemployment, with much the same mechanism at work as then.

There are several points to note from this discussion. First, as in the UK, it does seem that in general wage inflation leads price inflation, and also coincides more closely with the unemployment series than does price inflation. Thus in the period 1950–70 there were five discernible peaks in the unemployment series, all of which corresponded with troughs in the wage inflation series, but only three with the price inflation series. In the same period there were just three clear troughs in the unemployment series, each of which coincided with a peak in the wage inflation series, but none of which did so in the price inflation series. Furthermore in two of the years when wage inflation peaked prices did so in the following year. Conversely there seems to be no case in this earlier period when prices led wages. Thus, again as with the UK, it seems probable that the inflationary mechanism in this earlier period was one where excess demand first affected wages, and these in the form of increased costs then led to an increase in prices.

Secondly, it is clear that unemployment, at least up to 1965, was much more volatile and higher than in the UK, even after taking account of the different bases upon which they are measured. Whether this represents successful demand management policies by the UK governments of the time is less clear. But it is certainly the case that they had been more able and perhaps more willing than their counterparts in the USA to take this line of action. A key reason for this difference lies with the difficulties administrations often encounter in putting speedy measures through Congress.

Finally we may note that, again as with the UK, the period can be divided into two, with the watershed occurring between 1966 and 1970. The first, or Phillips curve, period appears to conform well with traditional excess demand based theories. We have already noted that the peaks in the unemployment series correspond exactly with troughs in the wage inflation series. In addition, when over a prolonged period unemployment was relatively high, as, for example, in 1958–63, then the rate of wage increase tended to be small. However, the second period is one where quite clearly this mechanism no longer worked in the obvious way it used to do. Indeed, it almost seems as if the previous negative relationship had been replaced by a positive one. In addition, it is quite clear that levels of unemployment which once would have caused wage inflation to fall sharply no longer do so. One obvious response is to argue that the unemployment figures no longer mean what they used to.

The Changing Nature of Unemployment

As in the UK, several economists have attempted to explain the break in the Phillips curve by challenging the validity of unemployment as an unchanging measure of excess demand. There are several aspects to this challenge. First amongst them is that changes in the composition of the labour force have caused the unemployment rate now to be higher than it would have been ten or twenty years ago, even under the same basic economic conditions. The most important of these changes has been the large increase in the youth proportion of the labour force due to the maturing of the postwar baby boom. Because the young have a higher probability of being unemployed than older workers this would lead to increased unemployment. This is of course only a temporary factor, and one presumes that by the 1980s it should have declined in importance.

It has also been claimed that the increase in female participation rates has had similar effects, although this is questionable as the unemployment rate for adult women has generally been slightly less than the overall rate. Thus any increases in their share of the labour force should have tended to reduce unemployment. Studies by Cagan (1977) and Flaim (1979) have estimated that demographic factors have increased unemployment by between 0.68 per cent and 1.04 per cent.

Other researchers have studied the impact that unemployment insurance has had on unemployment. Thus Hamermesh (1977) has looked at twelve empirical studies and concluded that for those receiving unemployment insurance, the duration of unemployment is longer by about 2.5 weeks. He therefore concluded that the unemployment insurance system adds an extra 0.51 percentage points to the unemployment total. Since the mid-1950s the ratio of unemployment insurance to average weekly earnings has increased relatively little. More important has been the increased proportion of the labour force who are covered by the unemployment insurance system. Tella (1976), for example, has estimated that the supplemental Insurance Assistance Program of 1975, which extended coverage to many workers in seasonal industries, added 0.2 per cent to the unemployment rate.

Another common explanation for the current high levels of unemployment is the minimum wage law. Cagan has estimated that this increased the unemployment rate by 0.63 percentage points between 1956 and 1974. These estimates were based on an earlier study by Mincer (1976), which apparently took into account that the minimum wage laws could have caused withdrawals from the labour force, due to workers becoming discouraged, which would have caused the unemployment rate to fall slightly. Still other factors which have been examined include the growth of multi-worker families, from 38.3 per cent of families with members in the labour force in 1956 to 52.9 per cent in 1976. It is argued that an unemployed person may be under less financial pressures, and thus take longer in searching for a new job, if other members of the family are employed. Antos, Mellow and Triplett (1979) have calculated that this would increase the unemployment rate by a maximum of 0.12 per cent. Others have argued that mandatory work registration might change the measured unemployment rate because it forces people who were not previously looking for work to begin looking. Support for this can be found in the 1976 report by the Council of Economic Advisors, who noted that when welfare mothers were required to register for work, their specific unemployment rate increased from 5.7 per cent to 11.5 per cent. On the basis of this Cagan has estimated a 0.2 per cent increase in the overall unemployment rate.

Thus it can be seen that if we were to sum all these effects then unemployment could have increased, for these reasons alone, by up to 2.6 per cent. However, one should treat this estimate with scepticism. For, apart from the statistical problems that underlie each estimate, there has been a bias at work on economists. The incentive for this work has been the recent high levels of unemployment, coupled with the shift or breakdown of the Phillips curve. This has led economists to search for factors which could have caused this increase, in addition, or as an alternative, to excess demand ones. There has not been an equal incentive to search for factors, such as the growth in numbers and efficiency of employment agencies, which would have acted in the opposite direction.

But even if we were to accept that there has been some increase in the natural rate of unemployment, as there may well have been, this still does not resolve the paradoxes which surround the Phillips curve. However unemployment is measured, the fact remains that in the 1970s recessions have failed to have as large an impact on inflation as we would have expected based on previous experience. Neither can adjustments to the unemployment rate explain why the close correlation between the peaks and troughs in unemployment and wage inflation, which we noted prior to 1969, disappears in the 1970s. Finally, we would note that many of the adjustments to unemployment would have a gradual impact over a twenty-year period. But the change in the Phillips curve relationship was a relatively sudden one. There is nothing in any of these adjustments which can even begin to explain that.

Explaining Inflation in the United States

To date we have established that the postwar period can be divided into two, with the watershed lying between 1966 and 1969. Prior to this the traditional Phillips curve seems to work well, whereas after it, it seems to break down entirely. This is a very similar pattern of events to that observed in the UK, and if it is to be explained in terms of the competitive wage no longer satisfying workers' aspirations, then we should also expect to see a similar increase in strike activity as in the UK. Unfortunately data on wage strikes are only available for the period beginning in 1964. These and data on all strikes are shown in Figure 4.5, which shows a very large increase in strike activity beginning in about 1966. If, for example, we take as a dividing line 5,000 strikes, then we can see that in the period up to 1967 strikes exceeded this figure in only two years, whereas in the period 1968–77 this level of strike activity was exceeded in every year. Thus the strike data are consistent with the synthesis we developed earlier. This indicates that much of the period since 1968 has been one where trade unions wished to secure wage increases in excess of that which employers wished to give. This, according to the theory, should also reflect a situation where this latter wage was based not on search theoretic considerations, but on the employer's desire to appear fair. The wage he will wish to pay on these implicit contract grounds will still vary with unemployment. For as this increases, then so will the cost of appearing fair, and the employer may decide to be a little less fair. But this responsiveness will be much less than in the search theoretic case, and this is why the Phillips curve relationship has been much more difficult to detect during this period.

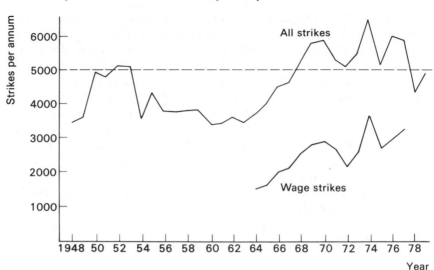

Figure 4.5   *Strikes in the US*
Sources: *Handbook of Labour Statistics* and *Analysis of Work Stop-pages*, various issues

If we now ask why this occurred at this time, then at first there is no obvious answer. After all, prior to this the USA had not been in a recession, neither was there an incomes policy in operation, to hold back the workers' standard of living. However, we may again gain some insight by looking at what happened to workers' disposable income in this period. Figure 4.6 shows the spendable average weekly earnings of a worker with three dependants. Here we can see that there was a fairly uniform growth in this throughout the 1950s and into the early 1960s. We can also see that this comes to a fairly abrupt end in about 1967. Indeed during the six-year period 1965–70, spendable earnings actually fell from $91.67 to $90.20. Thus by 1970 workers' actual wages were probably considerably below their aspirations. The onset of the recession would have reduced the wage the employer would want to pay, on pure search grounds, to well below that sufficient to satisfy those aspirations. Hence implicit contract considerations would become dominant in determining the wage employers would want to pay. This then is why the relationship between unemployment and inflation fundamentally changed at this time.

We now turn to a very real difference between the USA and the UK. Spendable average weekly earnings in the USA in the 1970s have not increased in line with previous trends. Instead they have remained virtually

constant. This reflects one of the basic differences between the two economies, that is, the differing power of the trade union movements. This is
very much larger and stronger in the UK, and has been largely able to
secure increases in line with workers' aspirations. In the USA this has not
been the case, and apart from a relatively small unionised sector, wages
have been determined largely on implicit contract grounds. In effect this

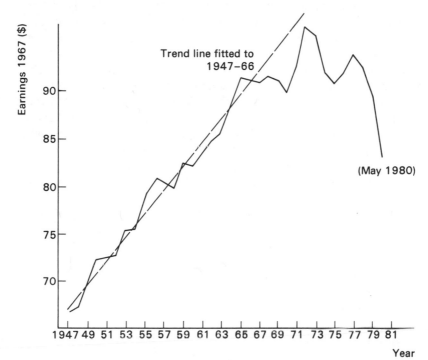

Figure 4.6   *Real spendable average weekly earnings in the US for worker*
with three dependants
Sources: *Handbook of Labour Statistics* and *Monthly Labour Review*
various issues

seems to have resulted in wage levels which have kept real net earnings
roughly constant, rather than on the previous upward trend. Apart from
1980 the one major exception to this appears to be the sharp increases in
1971–2. These correspond closely with the period of wage and price controls, and we may perhaps link the two together. This would then go some
way to explain the opposition of business to these controls.

There is just one further paradox to consider, and that is why union
membership seems to have fallen in recent years. We noted when dis-

cussing the UK that union membership had increased and we attributed this to workers in non-union establishments joining unions as a defensive measure. Why then did not the same thing happen in the USA? Why did workers not attempt to unionise upon discovering that employers were suddenly no longer willing to pay wages that would satisfy their aspirations? We can only speculate upon this, but it may be connected with the fact that trade unions have more legal rights and are much stronger economically and culturally in the UK. We can also speculate that employers' hostility to trade unions increased markedly after 1970, when suddenly they were demanding wages in excess of what the employers wished to pay. As a consequence they would have been keener to prevent unionisation, and if possible to de-unionise their firms. Because of organised labour's relative weakness in the USA they seem to have had some success in this. This hypothesis is also borne out by the fact that strikes of all kinds, not just over wages, have been increasing, and many trade union negotiators, employers and commentators have spoken of the increased bitterness of labour–management relations in recent years.

Before ending this section on the USA, I would make one final observation, which has some relevance for inflation in the early 1980s. Following the latest round of oil price increases, real spendable earnings in 1980 are lower than at any time since the early 1960s. This will have several effects. First, it is likely to strain industrial relations still further. Secondly, we can expect very large wage increases over the next few years, as employers attempt to protect their image of fairness by restoring real earnings to near previous levels.

Policy Implications

An examination of the policy implications is obviously an important part of any theory. None the less I feel some reticence in doing this, for several reasons. First, the theory is a first attempt to provide a unified theory of inflation, linking together parts of economic theory that were previously regarded as separate, or even competitive. As such it is both incomplete and liable to modification, perhaps considerably so. It is incomplete in as much as we have largely approached the problem in a partial way, examining the wage equation as if it were somehow independent of the rest of the economy. Considerably more light will be shed on the whole inflationary process once we move to a general equilibrium approach, looking at how prices, unemployment, vacancies and profits are interrelated. It is only when we do this that the full implications of any policy will become clear.

Secondly, it has become apparent as we reviewed the literature how quickly accepted theories become discarded and policy conclusions reversed. This is important, for governments do base their policies on economic theories and on the advice of economists, even if the link is sometimes tenuous. The wrong policy advice can have very harmful effects on an economy and the general population. Thus although it may seem a long way from the pages of an academic book or journal to social distress, the economist cannot differentiate himself from the implications which might follow from some government basing its policies on his theories.

For these reasons, and especially as the theory I have set out is a new one, this section is going to be relatively short, limited more to explaining why standard policy strategies are likely to be unsuccessful, and only tentatively discussing an alternative strategy. In addition, I am not even certain that, at least for the UK, inflation can be permanently reduced, in which case economists and policy makers would be better employed learning to live with it, especially as in the past nearly all attempts at reducing it, besides failing, have had harmful side-effects.

Excess demand policies
Policies aimed at reducing the level of excess demand within the economy will reduce the wage the employer wishes to pay on pure search grounds. If this exceeds the wage sufficient to satisfy workers' aspirations, then this will reduce inflation. Thus if inflation is caused by employers attempting to attract and retain labour in tight labour markets, then reducing the level of demand will reduce the rate of inflation. However, if this is not the case then the analysis is more complex. Let us take the situation where the employer is bargaining with a union, as is typically the case in the UK. There seems no reason to suppose, in ordinary circumstances, that this will reduce the worker's aspiration wage, although it may be one of the tactical considerations the trade union leader takes into account when deciding whether to risk a strike in furtherance of a wage claim. But this will not have any permanent effect as the union leader cannot go on indefinitely disappointing the aspirations of his membership. Hence we would not, in general, expect the union's target wage to be reduced by increasing unemployment. There may, however, be some impact upon the bargaining process itself. The widening gap between the wage the employer wishes to pay and the union leader's target wage may well increase the likelihood of a strike, which will reduce the union's target wage in the manner discussed in Chapter 2. This is especially so as profits are likely to be low in a recession, and thus the costs of a strike will be small in relative terms. But it is problematical as to how much the strike will serve to reduce the union leader's target wage.

Against this possibility there are others which will tend to work in the opposite direction. Most obvious is that with the reduction in demand will go a reduction in overtime working and opportunities for bonus payments, which will reduce workers' net incomes. They may attempt to compensate for this by an increase in their basic wages. Related to this is a factor which stems from the possibility that consumption plans will be based, not on individual income, but on household income. Increasing unemployment is liable to affect secondary workers in particular. Thus, for example, if the wife's income is lost, her husband may partially attempt to compensate for this by increasing his own income, via an increase in his wage rate.

There is, however, the possibility of a level of unemployment so high as to have a direct effect on workers' aspiration wages, due to fear of becoming and staying unemployed. But the effect must either be a permanent one, so that inflation will not reappear once demand is stimulated, or the level of unemployment must remain high for a sufficiently long enough time for expectations of further income growth to have fallen out of the permanent income calculations. The latter is not really practical, and it is the former possibility which the present UK government must be hoping will occur. Whether it will or not we do not as yet know. But if it does not then it will be clear that excess demand is no longer a viable weapon to use against inflation, in an economy with strong unions and where the target wage is in excess of the competitive wage. In particular this will still be so even if the government is willing to follow such policies to extreme lengths.

This is not the case in the USA, but even here excess demand will be a less efficient weapon to use against inflation than previously. For now the employer will be giving wage increases based on implicit contract rather than search considerations, which we have seen in practice roughly entails keeping real net earnings constant. Reducing demand may have some effect on this wage in as much as it increases the cost of appearing to be a fair employer, and the employer may then decide to be slightly less fair. But the effect on inflation is likely to be much smaller than when it is determined by pure search factors. We would probably therefore reject this as a method for reducing inflation, due to the excessive costs in terms of forgone output, provided that there are other policy options open.

I should emphasise here that I include amongst excess demand policies, monetarist ones. For it seems to me that it is through excess demand in the labour market that such policies have their principal effect on inflation. This can be illustrated with respect to the UK in 1980. A fairly rigid monetary policy is causing interest rates to be high, thus deterring investment. The value of the pound is also being kept artificially high partly because funds are being attracted to London by these high interest rates.

This in turn is making Britain's industries uncompetitive. It is these two effects together which are causing many firms either to go into liquidation, or contract by laying off workers. It is this which I believe is increasing unemployment, rather than, as monetarists would argue, people's expectations about inflation being in error at some time in the present or past.

Incomes policies

Let us again begin with the UK economy where trade unions are a major factor. We have seen that there have been many attempts at controlling incomes, but none have been permanently successful. The problems would seem to arise when the target wage exceeds the competitive wage. In this case, for inflation to be reduced permanently by the incomes policy, it will have to reduce workers' aspiration wages. There may indeed be some favourable effects in that any reduction in income in one period will reduce the aspiration wage in future periods. But such a process will be slow, and several years of income restraint will probably be necessary before there has been a significant enough reduction in workers' aspiration wages. However, I do not believe that an incomes policy can successfully restrain incomes for a lengthy period. If the policy is voluntary then pressure will build up against union leaders who co-operate with such a policy, and I do not believe that they can successfully withstand such pressure. If they try to do so, we can expect support for rivals to the leadership, both formal and informal, to increase. Faced with this threat to their positions, trade union leaders must respond to their membership's wishes, or be replaced by leaders who will.

Neither can a compulsory policy be successful, for there are a number of workers, in both the public and private sectors, with the strength to overcome any incomes policy. Furthermore, in a democracy it is probably unfeasible to hold down aggregate wages by controlling the incomes of only a part of the workforce, with the other part enjoying an ever increasing standard of living. This is not to deny that certain incomes policies have met with some temporary success, but in general this has also generated opposition to the policy which has led to its termination, after which inflation accelerates as workers attempt to restore their standard of living.

The USA has also seen several attempts at incomes policies, and, as in the UK, they have not been greeted with any great acclaim. The problems posed by unions' resistance, although less severe than in the UK, are still present. Oddly enough, however, additional problems arise due to the lack of widespread unionisation. In the UK incomes policies are relatively easy to enforce due to the tendency towards centralised pay bargaining. In the USA this is less so, and any comprehensive policy would take a large organisation to enforce. As a consequence the majority of incomes policies have concentrated on major wage bargains. They also tend to be accompanied by price controls, it being politically difficult to carry out one without the other, but these tend to be unpopular with the business community. Apart from these considerations however I believe that a compulsory incomes policy might have more chance of success in the USA than in the UK, though the degree of control that would be necessary would be cumbersome, involve resource misallocation, and be contrary to American philosophy. This last point is important. A belief in the free market system is very strong in the USA. A semi-permanent incomes policy would represent a significant departure from this system towards a form of state control, which is unlikely to be politically acceptable at this time.

Tax-based incomes policies
This is a special form of incomes policy first proposed several years ago by Wallich and Weintraub (1971). They proposed to levy a surcharge on the corporate profits tax for firms granting wage increases in excess of some guidepost figure. This would (for the USA) apply to all firms paying corporate income tax, with a possible exemption for small corporations. It would be narrower in scope than that of the wage controls in effect during the period 1971–4, and would exclude many small firms in construction and trucking, both of these being high wage and strong union industries. An alternative version proposed by Okun (1977) suggested giving tax relief incentives to workers and businessmen who enlisted in a co-operative anti-inflation effort.

There are several points to note about these proposals. First, they get around the tricky question of whether the incomes policy should be voluntary or compulsory. In addition, a tax-based incomes policy (TIP) has more flexibility than either. If expanding industries desperately want to attract additional labour, then they are still able to increase wages. Secondly, the philosophy behind these proposals is often regarded as one of increasing employers' resistance to union demands, although there seems to be no reason why they should not be equally, or even more, effective when inflation is being caused by excess demand in the labour market.

For the UK there seems little possibility that a TIP aimed at increasing employers' resistance to union demands will have much effect. Profits have been falling for many years; yet, excluding the most recent period, there seems little sign that employers have been able to resist union demands for increased wages, and in effect increased real wages. If this is so then a TIP would merely further squeeze profits, without necessarily having any marked effect on inflation. For the USA this is not the case, provided of course that the coverage was extensive enough, although not for the reasons Wallich and Weintraub thought likely. I have argued that inflation is being perpetuated mainly by employers taking into consideration implicit contract factors. In attempting to appear as fair employers, they have tended to maintain real net earnings at a constant level. This means that the oil price increases, instead of having a once and for all effect, have had continuing effects for several years. A TIP would increase the cost to the employer of appearing fair and hence help to minimise these further effects.

Conclusions
The problems facing the USA are much less daunting than those potentially facing the UK. In fact I do not really feel that the USA has an inflation problem as such. I regard the present problems as being caused by a combination of successive oil price increases and employers attempting to maintain real wages due to implicit contract considerations. Thus the impetus to inflation comes from successive oil price increases, and as such is exogenous to the American economy. As the effects of these are countered then inflation will gradually subside, with employers able to maintain real wages with successively lower money wage increases due to productivity growth. The key to America's problem therefore lies with the energy crisis. There are several possibilities. First, the USA will become more energy efficient, thereby reducing the effects of any future oil price increases. Secondly, alternative energy sources will be developed, including alternative oil sources, such as the North Sea. This will then help to reduce the upward pressures on the price of oil. Given this standpoint the optimal policy for the USA would seem to be to concentrate on problems other than inflation, such as unemployment, the quality of life, etc. There seems to be little that is positive, besides energy policies and perhaps a TIP, which policy makers can do to accelerate the return to normal inflation rates, but as in the UK the costs of trying may be high.

For the UK the problems are potentially much more severe. Oil price increases have been an important factor in Britain's current inflationary problem, but they have not been the most important. The ability of organised labour to achieve for their membership an ever increasing standard of living lies at the heart of the problem, and will continue to fuel inflation even when the energy problem recedes. If I am right in this then there are three possible policy options: reduce the unions' bargaining power, reduce workers' aspirations upon which the target wage is based, or increase the productive capacity of the economy so that the sum of these aspirations can be met without increasing prices. Of these options I believe that the first can only be achieved, if at all, at a large cost in terms of industrial harmony, strikes and perhaps freedom. The second possibility is one I find more attractive, but have doubts as to whether it can be achieved. As was made clear earlier, it is perhaps unlikely that either incomes policies or high unemployment can be maintained for a sufficiently long period to have any lasting effect on aspirations. However, the final option is perhaps a more viable proposition. A gradual reflation of the economy would increase opportunities for both overtime and secondary workers, both of which will increase household income. In addition everything should be done to increase the level of productivity growth. Again this is something about which it is easier to write about than achieve. In addition, as a policy prescription it is hardly novel; most economists who have studied the UK's problems in recent years have pointed to faster productivity growth as a necessary component of any solution to those problems. I have no unique insights to offer on how this may be achieved, but I can perhaps see some new hope in this direction. We are on the dawn of a new age of technology of which the micro-chip is just a part. This new technology offers the possibility of a more rapid increase in productivity than anything yet experienced in our history. If this is so then it may be that this is the means by which workers' aspirations can be met and therefore the problem of inflation solved. This is not to deny that this new technology may bring other social and economic problems in its wake. But the possibility remains that this may still offer the best hope that Britain has of permanently reducing inflation. Yet even so the process will be a slow one and widespread indexation of all money contracts should be introduced, both to minimise any harmful effects during this transition period and as an insurance policy in case price stability proves impossible to achieve.

Bibliography

Akerlof, G. (1980), A theory of social custom, of which unemployment may be one consequence, *Quarterly Journal of Economics*, vol. 94, pp. 749–75.

Akerlof, G. and Miyazaki, H. (1980), 'The implicit contract theory of unemployment meets the wage bill argument'. *Review of Economic Studies*, vol. 47, pp. 321–38.

Ando, A. and Modigliani, F. (1963), 'The "life cycle" hypothesis of saving: Aggregate implications and tests', *American Economic Review*, vol. 53, pp. 55–84.

Antos, J., Mellow, W. and Triplett, J. E. (1979), 'What is a current equivalent to unemployment rates of the past', *Monthly Labour Review*, vol. 102, pp. 36–46.

Ashenfelter, O. C. and Johnson, G. E. (1969), 'Bargaining theory, trade unions and industrial strike activity', *American Economic Review*, vol. 59, pp. 35–49.

Azariadis, C. (1975), 'Implicit contracts and under employment equilibria', *Journal of Political Economy*, vol. 83, pp. 1183–202.

Baily, M. N. (1974), 'Wages and employment under uncertain demand', *Review of Economic Studies*, vol. 41, pp. 119–55.

Barro, R. J. (1976), 'Rational expectations and the role of monetary policy', *Journal of Monetary Economics*, vol. 2, pp. 1095–117.

Barro, R. J. (1977), 'Unanticipated money growth and unemployment in the United States', *American Economic Review*, vol. 67, pp. 101–15.

Blanchard, O.-J. (1976). 'The non-transition to rational expectations', unpublished manuscript, Department of Economics, MIT.

Bowers, J. K., Cheshire, P. C., and Webb, A. E. (1970), 'The change in the relationship between unemployment and earnings increase: A review of some possible explanations', *National Institute Economic Review*, No. 54, pp. 44–63.

Bowlby, R. L. and Schriver, W. R. (1978), 'Bluffing and the "split the difference" theory of wage bargaining', *Industrial and Labour Relations Review*, vol. 31, pp. 161–71.

Brunner, K., Cukierman, A. and Meltzer, A. H. (1980), 'Stagflation, persistent unemployment and the permanence of economic shocks', *Journal of Monetary Economics*, vol. 6, pp. 467–92.

Buiter, W. H. (1980), 'The macroeconomics of Dr Pangloss: A critical survey of the new classical macroeconomics', *Economic Journal*, vol. 90, pp. 34–50.

Cagan, P. (1956), 'The dynamics of hyperinflation', in M. Friedman (ed.), *Studies in the Quantity Theory of Money* (Chicago: Chicago University Press), pp. 25–117.

Cagan, P. (1977), 'The reduction of inflation and the magnitude of unemployment', in W. Fellner (ed.), *Contemporary Economic Problems, 1977* (Washington, D.C.: American Enterprise Institute), pp. 15–52.

Calvo, G. A. and Phelps, E. S. (1977), 'Employment contingent wage contracts', in K. Brunner and A. H. Meltzer (eds.), *Stabilisation of the Domestic and International Economy*, Carnegie-Rochester Conference Series, vol. 5 (Amsterdam: North Holland), pp. 160–8.

Carlson, J. A. (1975), 'Are price expectations normally distributed?', *Journal of the American Statistical Association*, vol. 70, pp. 749–54.

Carlson, J. A. (1977), 'A study of price forecasts', *Annals of Economic and Social Measurement*, vol. 6, pp. 27–56.

Carlson, J. and Parkin, M. (1975), 'Inflation expectations', *Economica*, vol. 42, pp. 123–38.

Chow, G. C. (1975), *Analysis and Control of Dynamic Economic Systems* (New York: Wiley).

Clark, K. B. and Summers, L. H. (1979), 'Labour market dynamics and unemployment: A reconsideration', *Brookings Papers on Economic Activity*, No. 1, pp. 13–60.

Classen, K. P. (1977), 'The effects of unemployment insurance on the duration of unemployment and subsequent earnings', *Industrial and Labour Relations Review*, vol. 30, pp. 438–44.

Cripps, F. and Godley, W. (1976), 'A formal analysis of the Cambridge economic policy group model', *Economica*, vol. 43, pp. 335–48.

Cubbin, J. S. and Foley, K. (1977), 'The extent of benefit induced unemployment in Great Britain, some new evidence', *Oxford Economic Papers*, vol. 29, pp. 128–40.

Cyert, R. M. and DeGroot, M. H. (1974), 'Rational expectations and Bayesian analysis', *Journal of Political Economy*, vol. 82, pp. 521–36.

Danforth, J. P. (1979), 'On the role of consumption and decreasing absolute risk aversion in the theory of job search', in S. A. Lippman and J. J. McCall (eds.) *Studies in the Economics of Search* (Amsterdam: North Holland), pp. 109–32.

Duesenberry, J. (1958), *Business Cycles and Economic Growth* (New York: McGraw-Hill).

Dunlop, J. (1950), *Wage Determination under Trade Unions*, 2nd edn (New York: Augustus M. Kelley).

Eckstein, O. and Brinner, R. (1972), *The inflation process in the United States*, United States Joint Economic Committee of Congress, 2nd session (Washington, D.C.: U.S. Government Printing Office).

Eckstein, O. and Wilson, T. A. (1962), 'The determination of money wages in American industry', *Quarterly Journal of Economics*, vol. 76, pp. 379–414.

Ehrenberg, R. G. and Oaxaca, R. L. (1976), 'Unemployment insurance, duration of unemployment and subsequent gain', *The American Economic Review*, vol. 66, pp. 754–66.

Elliot, R. F. (1976), 'The national wage round in the U.K.: A sceptical view', *Oxford Bulletin of Economics and Statistics*, vol. 38, pp. 179–201.

Exekial, M. (1938), 'The cobweb theorem', *Quarterly Journal of Economics*, vol. 52, pp. 255–80.

Farber, H. S. (1978), 'Bargaining theory, wage outcomes and the occurrence of strikes: An econometric analysis', *American Economic Review*, vol. 68, pp. 262–71.

Feige, E. L. and Pearce, D. K. (1976), 'Economically rational expectations: are innovations in the rate of inflation independent of innovations in measures of monetary and Fiscal policy?', *Journal of Political Economy*, vol. 84, pp. 499–522.

Feldstein, M. (1976), 'Temporary layoffs in the theory of unemployment', *Journal of Political Economy*, vol. 84, pp. 937–57.

Feldstein, M. (1978), 'The effect of unemployment insurance on temporary layoff unemployment', *American Economic Review*, vol. 68, pp. 834–46.

Fischer, S. (1977), 'Long term contracts, rational expectations and the optimal money supply', *Journal of Political Economy*, vol. 85, pp. 191–205.

Fisher, I. (1926), 'A statistical relationship between unemployment and price changes', *International Labour Review*; reprinted as 'I discovered the Phillips curve', *Journal of Political Economy*, vol. 81 (1973), pp. 496–502.

Flaim, P. O. (1979), 'The effect of demographic changes on the nation's unemployment rate', *Monthly Labour Review*, vol. 102, pp. 13–23.

Flanagan, R. J. (1976), 'Wage interdependence in unionized labor markets', *Brookings Papers on Economic Activity*, no. 3, pp. 635–73.

Fleming, J. S. (1976), *Inflation* (Oxford: Oxford University Press).

Foster, J. I. and Gregory, M. (1977), 'Inflation expectations: the use of qualitative survey data', *Applied Economics*, vol. 9, pp. 319–29.

Friedman, B. M. (1979), 'Optimal expectations and the extreme information assumption of "rational expectations" macromodels', *Journal of Monetary Economics*, vol. 5, pp. 23–41.

Friedman, M. (1957), *Theory of the Consumption Function* (Princeton, N.J.: Princeton University Press).

Friedman, M. (1968), 'The role of monetary policy', *American Economic Review*, vol. 58, pp. 1–17.

Friedman, M. (1975), *Unemployment versus Inflation? An Evaluation of the Phillips Curve*, IEA Occasional Paper no. 44 (London: Institute of Economic Affairs).

Friedman, M. (1977), 'Nobel lecture: Inflation and unemployment', *Journal of Political Economy*, vol. 85, pp. 451–72.

160   *Inflation: A Theoretical Survey and Synthesis*

Garberino, J. W. (1962), *Wage Policy and Long Term Contracts* (Washington: Brookings).
Godfrey, L. (1971). 'The Phillips curve: incomes policy and trade union effects', in H. G. Johnson and A. R. Nobay (eds.), *The Current Inflation* (London: Macmillan), pp. 99–124.
Godfrey, L. and Taylor, J. (1973), 'Earnings changes in the U.K. 1954–70: Excess labour supply, expected inflation and union influence', *Oxford Bulletin of Economics and Statistics*, vol. 35, pp. 197–216.
Goldthorpe, J. H. (1978), 'The current inflation: towards a sociological account', in F. Hirsch and H. Goldthorpe (eds.), *The Political Economy of Inflation* (London: Martin Robertson), pp. 186–214.
Gordon, R. J. (1970), 'The recent acceleration of inflation and its lessons for the future', *Brookings Papers on Economic Activity*, no. 1, pp. 8–41.
Gordon, R. J. (1971), 'Inflation in recession and recovery', *Brookings Papers on Economic Activity*, no. 1, pp. 105–58.
Gordon, R. J. (1977a), 'Can the inflation of the 1970s be explained?', *Brookings Papers on Economic Activity*, no. 1, pp. 253–77.
Gordon, R. J. (1977b), 'Recent developments in the theory of inflation and unemployment', in E. Lundberg (ed.), *Inflation Theory and Anti Inflation Policy* (London: Macmillan), pp. 42–71.
Granger, C. W. J. (1969), 'Investigating causal relations by econometric models and cross-spectral methods', *Econometrica*, vol. 37, pp. 424–38.
Grossman, H. I. (1978), 'Risk shifting, layoffs and seniority', *Journal of Monetary Economics*, vol. 4, pp. 661–86.
Hall, J. R., Lippman, S. A. and McCall, J. J. (1979), 'Expected utility maximising job search', in S. A. Lippman and J. J. McCall (eds.), *Studies in the Economics of Search* (Amsterdam: North Holland), pp. 133–56.
Hall, R. E. (1975), 'The rigidity of wages and the persistence of unemployment', *Brookings Papers on Economic Activity*, no. 2, pp. 301–35.
Hall, R. E. (1980), 'Employment fluctuations and wage rigidity', *Brookings Papers on Economic Activity*, no. 1, pp. 91–123.
Hall, R. E. and Lilien, D. M. (1979), 'Efficient wage bargains under uncertain supply and demand', *American Economic Review*, vol. 69, pp. 868–79.
Hamermesh, D. S. (1973), 'Who wins in wage bargaining?', *Industrial and Labour Relations Review*, vol. 26, pp. 1146–9.
Hamermesh, D. S. (1977), *Jobless Pay and the Economy* (Baltimore: The Johns Hopkins University Press).
Hansen, A. (1921), 'Cycles of strikes', *American Economic Review*, vol. 11, pp. 616–21.
Harsanyi, J. C. (1956), 'Approaches to the bargaining problem before and after the theory of games', *Econometrica*, vol. 24, pp. 144–57.
Henry, S. G. B., Sawyer, M. C. and Smith, P. (1976), 'Models of inflation

in the United Kingdom: An evaluation', *National Institute Economic Review*, no. 77, pp. 60–71.

Hibbs, D. A. (1976), 'Industrial conflict in advanced societies', *American Political Science Review*, vol. 70, pp. 1033–58.

Hicks, J. R. (1946), *Value and Capital*, 2nd edn (Oxford: The Clarendon Press).

Hicks, J. R. (1963), *The Theory of Wages*, 2nd edn (London: Macmillan).

Hiller, E. A. (1969), *The Strike: A Study in Collective Action* (New York: Arno Press).

Hines, A. G. (1964), 'Trade unions and wage inflation in the United Kingdom: 1893–1961', *Review of Economic Studies*, vol. 31, pp. 221–52.

Hines, A. G. (1971), 'The determinants of the rate of change of money wage rates and the effectiveness of incomes policy', in H. G. Johnson and A. R. Nobay (eds), *The Current Inflation* (London: Macmillan), pp. 143–75.

Hirsch, F. (1978), 'The ideological underlay of inflation', in F. Hirsch and J. H. Goldthorpe (eds), *The Political Economy of Inflation* (London: Martin Robertson), pp. 263–84.

Hirsch, F. and Goldthorpe, J. H. (eds) (1978), *The Political Economy of Inflation* (London: Martin Robertson).

Holen, A. (1977), 'The effects of unemployment insurance entitlements on duration and job search outcome', *Industrial and Labour Relations Review*, vol. 30, pp. 445–50.

Holt, C. C. (1970), 'Job search, Phillips' wage relation and union influence: Theory and evidence', in E. S. Phelps et al., *Microeconomic Foundations of Employment and Inflation Theory* (New York: W. W. Norton), pp. 224–56.

Hudson, J. (1978), 'Expectations of wage inflation and their formation', *Applied Economics*, vol. 10, pp. 195–202.

Jacobs, R. L. and Jones, R. A. (1980), 'Price expectations in the United States, 1947–75', *American Economic Review*, vol. 70, pp. 269–77.

Johnson, G. E. (1977), 'The determination of wages in the unionised and non unionised sectors', *The British Journal of Industrial Relations*, vol. 15, pp. 211–25.

Johnston, J. (1972), 'A model of wage determination under bilateral monopoly', *Economic Journal*, vol. 82, pp. 837–52.

Johnston, J. and Timbrell, M. (1973), 'Empirical tests of a bargaining theory of wage rate determination', *Manchester School*, vol. 61, pp. 141–67.

Kalman, R. E. (1960), 'A new approach to linear filtering and prediction problems', *Journal of Basic Engineering, Trans.*, vol. 82, pp. 33–45.

Kasper, H. (1967), 'The asking price of labor and the duration of unemployment (in Minnesota)', *Review of Economics and Statistics*, vol. 49, pp. 165–72.

Kiefer, N. and Neumann, G. (1979), 'An empirical job search model with a test of the constant reservation wage hypothesis', *Journal of Political Economy*, vol. 87, pp. 89–108.

Knobl, A. (1974), 'Price expectations and actual price behaviour in Germany', *International Monetary Fund Staff Papers*, vol. 21. pp. 83–100.

Krech, D. and Crutchfield, R. S. (1948), *Theory and Problems of Social Psychology* (New York: McGraw-Hill).

Laidler, D. E. W. (1981), 'Monetarism: An interpretation and an assessment', *Economic Journal*, vol. 91. pp. 1–28.

Laidler, D. E. W. and Parkin, J. M. (1975), 'Inflation: A survey', *Economic Journal*, vol. 85, pp. 741–809.

Lilien, D. M. (1980), 'The cyclical pattern of temporary layoffs in United States manufacturing', *Review of Economics and Statistics*, vol. 62, pp. 24–31.

Lippman, S. A. and McCall, J. J. (1976), 'The economics of job search: A survey, Part 1', *Economic Inquiry*, vol. 14, pp. 155–89.

Lipsey, R. G. (1960), 'The relationship between unemployment and the rate of change of money wage rates in the UK, 1862–1957: A further analysis', *Economica*, vol. 27, pp. 1–31.

Lipsey, R. G. (1978), 'The place of the Phillips curve in macroeconomic models', in A. R. Bergstrom, A. J. L. Catt, M. H. Peston and B. D. J. Silversone (eds), *Stability and Inflation* (Chichester: Wiley), pp. 49–76.

Lipsey, R. G. and Steur, M. D. (1961), 'The relation between profits and wage rates', *Economica*, vol. 28, pp. 137–55.

Lowe, J. (1822), *The Present State of England in Regard to Agriculture, Trade and Finance. With a Comparison of the Prospects of England and France* (London).

Lucas, R. E., Jr. (1972a), 'Econometric testing of the natural rate hypothesis', in O. Eckstein (ed.), *The Economics of Price Determination Conference* (Washington: Board of Governors, Federal Reserve System), pp. 50–9.

Lucas, R. E., Jr. (1972b), 'Expectations and the neutrality of money', *Journal of Economic Theory*, vol. 4, pp. 103–24.

Lucas, R. E., Jr. (1975), 'An economic model of the business cycle', *Journal of Political Economy*, vol. 83, pp. 1113–44.

Lucas, R. E., Jr. (1978), 'Unemployment policy', *American Economic Review*, papers and proceedings, vol. 68, pp. 353–7.

Lucas, R. E., Jr. and Rapping, L. A. (1969), 'Real wages, employment and inflation', *Journal of Political Economy*, vol. 77, pp. 721–54.

Malinvaud, E. (1977), *The Theory of Unemployment Reconsidered* (Oxford: Basil Blackwell).

Marshall, A. (1920), *The Principles of Economics*, 8th edn (London: Macmillan).

McCallum, B. T. (1976), 'Rational expectations and the natural rate hypothesis: some consistent estimates', *Econometrica*, vol. 44, pp. 43–52.

McCallum, B. T. (1979), 'The current state of the policy ineffectiveness debate', *American Economic Review*, papers and proceedings, vol. 69, pp. 240–5.

McGuire, T. W. (1976), 'Price change expectations and the Phillips curve', in K. Brunner and A. H. Meltzer (eds), *The Econometrics of Price and Wage Controls*, Carnegie-Rochester Conference Series vol. 2 (Amsterdam: North Holland), pp. 115–57.

Metzler, L. (1941), 'The nature and stability of inventory cycles', *Review of Economics and Statistics*, vol. 29, pp. 113–29.

Mincer, J. (1976), 'Unemployment effects of minimum wages', *Journal of Political Economy*, vol. 84, pp. 87–104.

Mitchell, D. J. B. (1978), 'Union wage determination: Policy implications and outlook', *Brookings Papers on Economic Activity*, no. 3, pp. 537–82.

Modigliani, F. and Grunberg, E. (1954), 'The predictability of social events', *Journal of Political Economy*, vol. 62, pp. 465–78.

Modigliani, F. and Sutch, R. J. (1966), 'Innovations in interest rate policy', *American Economic Review*, vol. 56, pp. 178–97.

Mortenson, D. T. (1970), 'Job search, the duration of unemployment and the Phillips curve', *American Economic Review*, vol. 60, pp. 847–62, reprinted in Phelps et al. (1970).

Mortenson, D. T. (1977), 'Unemployment insurance and job search decisions', *Industrial and Labour Relations Review*, vol. 30, pp. 505–17.

Mullineaux, D. J. (1980a), 'Unemployment, industrial production and inflation uncertainty in the United States', *Review of Economics and Statistics*, vol. 62, pp. 163–9.

Mullineaux, D. J. (1980b), 'Inflation expectations and money growth in the United States', *American Economic Review*, vol. 70, pp. 149–61.

Muth, J. F. (1960), 'Optimal properties of exponentially weighted forecasts', *Journal of the American Statistical Association*, vol. 55, pp. 299–306.

Muth, J. F. (1961), 'Rational expectations and the theory of price movements', *Econometrica*, vol. 29, pp. 315–35.

Myrdal, G. (1939), *Monetary Economics* (London: Hodge).

Nash, J. F., Jr. (1950), 'The bargaining problem', *Econometrica*, vol. 18, pp. 155–62.

Nash, J. F., Jr. (1953), 'Two person co-operative games', *Econometrica*, vol. 21, pp. 128–40.

Nelson, C. R. (1975), 'Rational expectations and the predictive efficiency of economic models', *Journal of Business*, vol. 48, pp. 331–43.

Nerlove, M. (1958), *The Dynamics of Supply: Estimation of Farmers' Responses to Price* (Baltimore: The Johns Hopkins University Press).

Nerlove, M. (1972), 'Lags in economic behaviour', *Econometrica*, vol. 40, pp. 221–51.

Nickell, S. (1979), 'The effect of unemployment and related benefits on the duration of unemployment', *Economic Journal*, vol. 89, pp. 34–9.

Okun, A. M. (1975), 'Inflation: its mechanics and welfare costs', *Brookings Papers on Economic Activity*, no. 2, pp. 351–90.

Okun, A. M. (1977), 'The great stagflation swamp', *Challenge*, vol. 20, pp. 6–13.

Panic, M. (1978), 'The origins of increasing inflationary tendencies in contemporary society', in F. Hirsch and J. H. Goldthorpe (eds), *The Political Economy of Inflation* (London: Martin Robertson).

Parkin, J. M., Sumner, M. T. and Ward, R. (1976), 'The effects of excess demand, generalised expectations and wage price controls on wage inflation in the UK: 1956–71', in K. Brunner and A. H. Meltzer (eds.), *The Economics of Price and Wage Controls*, Carnegie-Rochester Conference Series, vol. 2 (Amsterdam: North Holland). pp. 193–221.

Parsons, D. O. (1973), 'Quit rates over time: A search and information approach', *American Economic Review*, vol. 63, pp. 390–401.

Paunio and Suvanto, A. (1977), 'Changes in price expectations: Some tests using data on indexed and non indexed bonds', *Economica*, vol. 44, pp. 3–45.

Perry, G. L. (1970), 'Changing labour markets and inflation', *Brookings Papers on Economic Activity*, no. 3, pp. 411–39.

Perry, G. L. (1978), 'Slowing the wage-price spiral: The macroeconomic view', *Brookings Papers on Economic Activity*, no. 2, pp. 259–91.

Perry, G. L. (1980), 'Inflation in theory and practice', *Brookings Papers on Economic Activity*, no. 1, pp. 207–41.

Pesando, J. (1975), 'A note on the rationality of the Livingstone expectations data', *Journal of Political Economy*, vol. 83, pp. 849–58.

Phelps, E. S. (1968), 'Money wage dynamics and labour market equilibrium', *Journal of Political Economy*, vol. 76, pp. 678–711, reprinted in Phelps et al. (1970).

Phelps, E. S. et al. (1970), *Microeconomic Foundations of Employment and Inflation Theory* (New York: W. W. Norton).

Phelps, E. S. (1977), 'Indexation issues: A comment on the Blinder and Fischer papers', in K. Brunner and A. H. Meltzer (eds.), *Stabilisation of the Domestic and International Economy*, Carnegie-Rochester conference series, vol. 5 (Amsterdam: North Holland), pp. 149–59.

Phelps, E. S. and Taylor, J. B. (1977), 'Stabilising properties of monetary policy under rational expectations', *Journal of Political Economy*, vol. 84, pp. 163–90.

Phillips, A. W. (1958), 'The relation between unemployment and the rate of change of money wages rates in the United Kingdom, 1861–1957', *Economica*, vol. 25, pp. 283–99.

Purdy, D. L. and Zis, G. (1973), 'On the concept and measurement of union militancy', in D. E. W. Laidler and D. L. Purdy (eds.), *Inflation and Labour Markets* (Manchester: Manchester University Press), pp. 38–60.

Riddel, W. C. (1979), 'The empirical foundations of the Phillips curve, evidence from Canadian wage contract data', *Econometrica*, vol. 47, pp. 1–24.

Rose, D. E. (1972), 'A general error-learning model of expectation formation', University of Manchester Inflation Workshop, Discussion Paper no. 7210.

Ross, A. M. (1948), *Trade Union Wage Policy* (Berkeley: University of California Press).

Rothschild, M. (1974), 'Searching for the lowest price when the distribution of prices is unknown', *Journal of Political Economy*, vol. 82, pp. 689–711.

Rowley, J. C. R. and Wilton, D. A. (1973), 'Quarterly models of wage determination, some new efficient estimates', *American Economic Review*, vol. 63, pp. 380–9.

Rowley, J. C. R. and Wilton, D. A. (1974), 'The sensitivity of quarterly models of wage determination to aggregation assumptions', *Quarterly Journal of Economics*, vol. 88, pp. 671–80.

Runciman, W. G. (1966), *Relative Deprivation and Social Justice* (London: Routledge & Kegan Paul).

Salop, S. C. (1973), 'Systematic job search and unemployment', *Review of Economic Studies*, vol. 40, pp. 191–201.

Samuelson, P. A. and Solow, R. M. (1960), 'Analytical aspects of anti inflation policy', *American Economic Review*, papers and proceedings, vol. 50, pp. 177–94.

Sargan, J. D. (1964), 'Wages and prices in the United Kingdom: A study in econometric methodology', in P. E. Hart, G. Mills and J. K. Whitaker (eds.), *Econometric Analysis for National Economic Planning* (London: Butterworth).

Sargan, J. D. (1971), 'A study of wages and prices in the UK 1949–1968', in H. G. Johnson and A. B. Nobay (eds.), *The Current Inflation* (London: Macmillan).

Sargent, T. J. (1973), 'Rational expectations, the real rate of interest and the natural rate of unemployment', *Brookings Papers on Economic Activity*, no. 2, pp. 429–72.

Sargent, T. J. (1976a), 'A classical macroeconomic model for the United States', *Journal of Political Economy*, vol. 84, pp. 207–37.

Sargent, T. J. (1976b), 'The observational equivalence of natural and unnatural rate theories of macroeconomics', *Journal of Political Economy*, vol. 84, pp. 631–40.

Sargent, T. J. and Wallace, N. (1973), 'Rational expectations and the dynamics of hyperinflation', *International Economic Review*, vol. 14, pp. 328–50.

Sargent, T. J. and Wallace, N. (1975). 'Rational expectations, the optimal monetary instrument and the optimal money supply rule', *Journal of Political Economy*, vol. 83, pp. 241–54.

Sargent, T. J. and Wallace, N. (1976), 'Rational expectations and the theory of economic policy', *Journal of Monetary Economics*, vol. 12, pp. 169–83.

Saunders, P. G. and Nobay, A. R. (1972), 'Price expectations, the Phillips curve and incomes policy', in J. M. Parkin and M. T. Sumner (eds), *Incomes Policy and Inflation* (Manchester: Manchester University Press).

Shackle, G. L. S. (1967), *The Years of High Theory* (Cambridge: Cambridge University Press).

Shiller, R. J. (1978), 'Rational expectations and the dynamic structure of macroeconomic models: A critical review', *Journal of Monetary Economics*, vol. 4, pp. 1–44.

Simler, N. J. and Tella, A. (1968), 'Labour reserves and the Phillips curve', *Review of Economics and Statistics*, vol. 50, pp. 32–49.

Solow, R. M. (1969), *Price Expectations and the Behaviour of the Price Level* (Manchester: Manchester University Press).

Solow, R. M. (1980), 'On theories of unemployment', *American Economic Review*, vol. 70, pp. 1–11.

Spence, M. (1973), 'Job market signalling', *Quarterly Journal of Economics*, vol. 87, pp. 355–74.

Stephenson, S. P., Jr. (1976), 'The economics of youth job search behaviour', *Review of Economics and Statistics*, vol. 58, pp. 104–11.

Stigler, G. J. (1962), 'Information in the labor market', *Journal of Political Economy*, vol. 72. pp. 94–105.

Taylor, J. (1970), 'Hidden unemployment, hoarded labour, and the Phillips curve', *Southern Economic Journal*, vol. 37, pp. 1–16.

Taylor, J. (1972), 'Incomes policy, the structure of unemployment and the Phillips curve: The United Kingdom experience: 1953–70', in J. M. Parkin and M. T. Sumner (eds), *Incomes Policy and Inflation* (Manchester: Manchester University Press), pp. 182–200.

Taylor, J. B. (1975), 'Monetary policy during a transition to rational expectations', *Journal of Political Economy*, vol. 83, pp. 1009–21.

Taylor, J. B. (1979), 'Staggered wage setting in a macro model', *American Economic Review*, vol. 69, pp. 108–13.

Taylor, L. (1970), 'The existence of optimal distributed lags', *Review of Economic Studies*, vol. 37, pp. 95–106.

Tella, A. (1976), 'Analyzing joblessness', *New York Times*, October 27.

Telser, L. G. (1973), 'Searching for the lowest price', *American Economic Review*, vol. 63, pp. 40–9.

Tobin, J. R. (1972), 'The wage price mechanism: overview of the conference', in O. Eckstein (ed.), *The Econometrics of Price Determination Conference* (Washington, D.C.: Federal Reserve System), pp. 5–15.

Topel, R. and Welch, F. (1980), 'Unemployment insurance: Survey and extensions', *Economica*, vol. 47, pp. 351–79.

Trevithick, J. A. and Mulvey, C. (1975), *The Economics of Inflation* (London: Martin Robertson).

Turnovsky, S. J. (1969), 'A Bayesian approach to the theory of expectations', *Journal of Economic Theory*, vol. 1, pp. 220–7.

Turnovsky, S. J. (1970), 'Empirical evidence on the formation of price expectations', *Journal of American Statistical Association*, vol. 65, pp. 1441–54.

Turnovsky, S. J. (1972), 'The expectations hypothesis and the aggregate wage equation: some empirical evidence for Canada', *Economica*, vol. 39, pp. 1–17.

Turnovsky, S. J. and Wachter, M. L. (1972), 'A test of the expectations hypothesis using directly observed wage and price expectations', *Review of Economics and Statistics*, vol. 54, pp. 47–54.

von Neumann, J. and Morgenstern, O. (1947), *Theory of Games and Economic Behaviour* (Princeton, N.J.: Princeton University Press).

Wallich, H. C. and Weintraub, S. (1971), 'A tax based incomes policy', *Journal of Economic Issues*, vol. 5, pp. 1–19.

Wallis, K. F. (1971), 'Wages, prices and incomes policies: some comments', *Economica*, vol. 38, pp. 304–10.

Wallis, K. F. (1980), 'Econometric implications of the rational expectations hypothesis', *Econometrica*, vol. 48, pp. 49–73.

Wilde, L. L. (1979), 'An information-theoretic approach to job quits', in S. A. Lippman and J. J. McCall (eds), *Studies in the Economics of Search* (Amsterdam: North Holland), pp. 35–52.

Wiles, P. (1973), 'Cost inflation and the state of economic theory', *Economic Journal*, vol. 83, pp. 377–98.

Williamson, J. and Wood, G. (1976), 'The British inflation: Indigenous or imported?', *American Economic Review*, vol. 66, pp. 520–31.

Zeuthan, F. (1930), *Problems of Monopoly and Economic Welfare* (London: Routledge).

Index